"The Object Lessons series achieves something very close to magic: the books take ordinary—even banal—objects and animate them with a rich history of invention, political struggle, science, and popular mythology. Filled with fascinating details and conveyed in sharp, accessible prose, the books make the everyday world come to life. Be warned: once you've read a few of these, you'll start walking around your house, picking up random objects, and musing aloud: 'I wonder what the story is behind this thing?'"

Steven Johnson, author of *Where Good Ideas Come From* and *How We Got to Now*

"Object Lessons describes themselves as 'short, beautiful books,' and to that, I'll say, amen. . . . If you read enough Object Lessons books, you'll fill your head with plenty of trivia to amaze and annoy your friends and loved ones—caution recommended on pontificating on the objects surrounding you. More importantly, though . . . they inspire us to take a second look at parts of the everyday that we've taken for granted. These are not so much lessons about the objects themselves, but opportunities for self-reflection and storytelling. They remind us that we are surrounded by a wondrous world, as long as we care to look."

John Warner, *The Chicago Tribune*

T0205067

OBJECT LESSONS

A book series about the hidden lives of ordinary things.

Series Editors:

Ian Bogost and Christopher Schaberg

Advisory Board:

Sara Ahmed, Jane Bennett, Jeffrey Jerome Cohen,
Johanna Drucker, Raiford Guins, Graham Harman,
renée hoogland, Pam Houston, Eileen Joy, Douglas
Kahn, Daniel Miller, Esther Milne, Timothy Morton,
Kathleen Stewart, Nigel Thrift, Rob Walker, Michele White.

In association with

Georgia Tech | Center for Media Studies

BOOKS IN THE SERIES

tumor

ANNA LEAHY

Bloomsbury Academic
An imprint of Bloomsbury Publishing Inc

B L O O M S B U R Y
NEW YORK • LONDON • OXFORD • NEW DELHI • SYDNEY

Bloomsbury Academic
An imprint of Bloomsbury Publishing Inc

1385 Broadway	50 Bedford Square
New York	London
NY 10018	WC1B 3DP
USA	UK

www.bloomsbury.com

BLOOMSBURY and the Diana logo are trademarks of Bloomsbury Publishing Plc

First published 2017

© Anna Leahy, 2017

Lucille Clifton, "1994" from *The Collected Poems of Lucille Clifton*.
Copyright © 1996
by Lucille Clifton. Reprinted with the permission of The Permissions
Company, Inc. on behalf of BOA Editions Ltd., www.boaeditions.org.

Library of Congress Cataloging-in-Publication Data
Names: Leahy, Anna, 1965- author.
Title: Tumor / Anna Leahy.
Other titles: Object Lesson
Description: New York, NY : Bloomsbury Academic, 2017. | Series: Object
lessons | Includes bibliographical references and index.
Identifiers: LCCN 2016055320 (print) | LCCN 2016055941 (ebook) | ISBN
9781501323300 (pbk. : alk. paper) | ISBN 9781501323324 (ePDF) | ISBN
9781501323317 (ePUB)
Subjects: | MESH: Neoplasms–psychology | Neoplasms–therapy | Health
Knowledge, Attitudes, Practice Classification: LCC RC263 (print) | LCC RC263 (ebook) |
NLM QZ 200 | DDC 616.99/4–dc23
LC record available at https://lccn.loc.gov/2016055320

ISBN: PB: 978-1-5013-2330-0
ePub: 978-1-5013-2331-7
ePDF: 978-1-5013-2332-4

Series: Object Lessons

Cover design: Alice Marwick

Typeset by Deanta Global Publishing Services, Chennai, India
Printed and bound in the United States of America

dedicated to the many whose journey
through life includes cancer

CONTENTS

1 TUMOR IN THE FAMILY

Mother

Early in 2012, my mother ended up in a hospital emergency room with symptoms indicative of a gallbladder attack. She had no history of gallbladder attacks but had been suffering sporadic nausea, fullness, and general fatigue for several months. The physician who read the x-ray of her abdomen confirmed a possible problem with her gallbladder but told her that it did not require immediate surgery. He told her to see a specialist right away. He was adamant about this referral in a way that got my mother's attention. In hindsight, we know that he had seen a shadow on her pancreas, an organ tucked near the intestines that produces a juice filled with digestive enzymes and several hormones (such as insulin). The word *pancreas* comes from the Greek meaning *entirely flesh*.[1] That shadow on the pancreas—on my mother's internal flesh—turned out to be a tumor, entirely her own tissue but somehow out of character, out of control.

Based on that initial x-ray, the specialist discussed the probability of cancer. After additional imaging, he inserted a lighted tube down my mother's throat, passed a needle through the tube, and removed cells from the tumor for testing. My mother was officially diagnosed with pancreatic cancer on March 1, when the results of the biopsy of the tumor on her pancreas revealed malignant cells. She was already sure of that diagnosis before then. She had talked with my sister and me about the online research she'd done. She gathered as much information as she could about what the tumor might be, and then she went over all her accounts, assets, and will.

According to the Pancreatic Cancer Action Network, a resource on which my mother, my sister, and I relied in gathering information early on in her illness, the chances of a patient surviving five years after the diagnosis of pancreatic cancer is just 8 percent. That's actually a recent uptick in survival, but "it is still the lowest survival rate of any major cancer."[2] The chance of surviving a full year from diagnosis is a pitiful 29 percent.[3] (It's even worse in the United Kingdom.[4]) When my mother read such numbers, she resigned herself to the likelihood that she would be dead within a year, at the age of seventy-two.

The future of pancreatic cancer looks even bleaker than the current state of this disease. Demographic populations change; the population in the United States is getting older, and age is the greatest risk factor for cancer. Treatment options evolve, usually in hopes of decreasing mortality rates, though the advances in treatment for pancreatic cancer seem meager. Incidence rates of this type of cancer are creeping upward, though no one is exactly sure why. And this cancer is often caught too late for existing treatment options to lower the death rate substantially. A study in the journal *Cancer Research* predicts that deaths from pancreatic cancer will increase "dramatically" and that pancreatic cancer will become the second leading cause of cancer death before 2030, supplanting breast cancer.[5]

Breast cancer is the most commonly diagnosed cancer in women, accounting for 29 percent of all cancer diagnoses. Women in the United States have a one-in-eight chance of such a diagnosis.[6] My mother had been treated for that cancer more than ten years before her pancreatic cancer diagnosis. The tumor in her breast was relatively small and was removed surgically. After recovering quickly from that lumpectomy, she underwent treatment with radiation and then took a daily dose of the oral medication anastrozole to lower her chance of recurrence of breast cancer, since recurrence would have been more threatening than the initial tumor that had been removed and treatment more drastic.

Some cancers are more prevalent in the general population than are others. The incidence rate of breast cancer is much higher than that of pancreatic cancer. The National Cancer Institute estimates a woman's lifetime risk of developing breast cancer at 12.3 percent,[7] whereas a person's lifetime risk of developing pancreatic cancer is 1.5 percent.[8] Many more women will face a breast cancer diagnosis than a diagnosis of pancreatic cancer. The mortality rate—the clinical term for *death rate,* a reminder of what being mortal means—of breast cancer, however, is much lower because breast cancer is more likely to be detected early, before the cancer has spread, and because treatment for this type of cancer is more effective. So, as cancers go, breast cancer is among the most common, and most people with breast cancer—89 percent—survive at least five years. Overall, 78 percent of breast cancer patients survive fifteen years or more. For someone in my mother's circumstances when she discovered the small lump, the five-year survival rate is 99 percent.[9] While many people—about 41,000 annually in the United States—die of breast cancer,[10] those odds are pretty good when it comes to cancer.

A friend who walked in a Race for the Cure event to raise money for breast cancer research a few years ago said that there were too many women to fit in the traditional photograph of survivors. The high incidence rate combined with the increasingly successful treatment of breast cancer has grown to the point that it could no longer be framed. It's easy to look at the numbers and think that having a small tumor removed from one's breast is like not having had cancer at all. But one woman in every hundred doesn't survive her tumor. Women with advanced disease or women with recurrences after the battle had supposedly been won can't strap on their sneakers and run past the disease.

One type of tumor is not just like another; each cancer has its own madness to its method. The number of deaths for pancreatic cancer is roughly the same as for breast cancer—almost 42,000 annually in the United States—but far fewer people will ever hear that they have pancreatic cancer. The vast majority people who do get that diagnosis do not live long, no matter what treatment they undergo. In a reverse perversity of statistics, 78 percent of breast cancer patients survive fifteen years from diagnosis, but about 80 percent of pancreatic cancer patients are dead in a year. In his Pulitzer Prize-winning book, *The Emperor of All Maladies*, physician Siddhartha Mukherjee admits how daunting this particular cancer can be for both physician and patient. "Even in oncology, a dismal discipline to begin with, this—unresected pancreatic cancer—was considered the epitome of the dismal."[11] *Dismal,* from the Latin meaning *unlucky days*, or the days when evil lashes out in your direction. Pancreatic cancer leads to bad days for everyone involved.

Jazz pianist Count Basie, composer Henry Mancini, opera singer Luciano Pavarotti, Pink Floyd's Syd Barrett, comedian Jack Benny, and actors Ann Francis, Rex Harrison, Pernell Roberts, Ben Gazzara, and Fred Gwynne all died of pancreatic cancer. After a couple of months of abdominal pain in 1991, actor Michael Landon of *Bonanza* (co-star Pernell Roberts was diagnosed much later) and *Little House on the Prairie* fame—staples of my childhood television viewing—was diagnosed with pancreatic cancer at the age of fifty-four; he lived less than three months. Bonnie Franklin, star of yet another favorite television show of my childhood, *One Day at a Time,* died of pancreatic cancer in March 2013, less than six months after the announcement that she was being treated. Actor Patrick Swayze of *Dirty Dancing* fame was diagnosed in

January 2008 and died in September 2009 at age fifty-seven. Julius Carry, a Chicago native who played Bruce Campbell's best-buddy bounty hunter on *The Adventures of Brisco County, Jr.* and Sho'nuff in the film *The Last Dragon,* died of pancreatic cancer in 2008 at the age of fifty-six.

Sally Ride, the first American woman in space, died the summer my mother was undergoing chemotherapy; Ride had been diagnosed seventeen months earlier. As I wrote this, another space shuttle astronaut, climate scientist Piers Sellers, was diagnosed and decided to spend as much time as he could on his work and with those he loves; he was

FIGURE 1.1 Mission Specialist Sally Ride on forward deck of space shuttle *Challenger* on June 21, 1983.
Source: NASA.

diagnosed in October 2015 and, the following January, said his prognosis was twelve to eighteen months.[12] He died on December 23, 2016, as prognosed.

Carnegie Mellon professor Randy Pausch was diagnosed in 2006 and underwent the Whipple procedure. A year later, he gave his "Last Lecture"—part of a series of previously hypothetical final talks by Carnegie Mellon professors— entitled "Really Achieving Your Childhood Dreams."[13] Pausch's talk has been watched by more than eighteen million people. In the wake of this sudden popularity, he testified before Congress about funding for cancer research, appeared on *The Oprah Winfrey Show* and in the film *Star Trek,* was a "Person of the Week" on ABC's news, and co-wrote a bestselling book that expanded the lecture. Pausch died at the age of forty-seven, less than two years after his diagnosis.

Apple computer whiz Steve Jobs announced in 2004, when he was forty-nine years old, that he had the lesser of the two evil forms of pancreatic cancer. He kept details of his health as private as possible and had a liver transplant in 2009. He lived until 2011. Supreme Court Justice Ruth Bader Ginsburg had a small pancreatic cancer tumor removed— resected through surgery—in 2009 and was treated for colorectal cancer ten years before that. As of this writing, Ginsburg is still deciding cases at age eighty-three.

As with breast cancer, the best chance of long-term survival of pancreatic cancer is surgical removal of the tumor. The surgery is one of two types. The simpler distal pancreatectomy and splenectomy can be done laparoscopically if the tumor is located at the body or tail of the pancreas. The Whipple procedure is done for tumors located at the head, neck, or uncinate (hooked) process. With the pancreas nestled next to the beginning of the small intestine that leaves the stomach, this operation takes several hours, during which organs and parts of organs are removed, and then what's left is reconnected in hopes of a semblance of normal life and a slightly higher chance of living longer. However, only 20 percent of those diagnosed with pancreatic cancer are eligible for surgery. Often, a person finds out she has pancreatic cancer only after it has metastasized, or spread elsewhere in the body, when surgical removal of the initial tumor won't help curb the progression of the disease nor halt the demise of the patient. Even with surgery, the majority of people who have pancreatic cancer do not survive five years. Mukherjee's patient Beatrice Sorenson, willing to try anything, had undergone surgery, radiation, and chemotherapy to treat the cancer of her pancreas. "But strong or not, there was nothing left to try."[14]

My mother's tumor, to her surprise, appeared to be operable, based on the CT scans, the more nuanced, cross-sectional x-ray imaging via computed tomography. She opted to undergo the drastic Whipple surgery in hopes of living a few years instead of a few months. Statistics, after all, are an extrapolation about the whole population and don't indicate whether a particular individual in question will live or die within a certain time frame. If the odds can be made better than dismal, why not give it a go?

After the surgeon had opened the abdomen, however, he discovered that the tumor, which was about the length across his closed fist and not as big as the pancreas itself, was attached to a large artery. Though the tumor had not broken through the artery, he could not pry the cancerous mass from that vital blood vessel. He told us that, had it been attached to a vein instead, he would have been able to sever the tumor from its perch and repair the vein. Even though the artery was at risk from tumor invasion, the body often adjusts to the tumor as it grows so that blood is rerouted. But he could not reroute the blood vessel with scalpel and suture. To sever an artery probably would have left the patient—my mother—dead on the table. So, he removed the problematic gallbladder, in case that would ease some symptoms, and closed her belly with the cancer still inside her.

Astronaut Sally Ride's surgeon must have faced similar dilemmas and disappointments when he performed surgery in October 2011, after several months of chemotherapy and radiation were used to shrink the tumor. Lynn Sherr, in her biography of Ride, notes that the cancer involved more blood vessels than the surgeon expected and that not all the disease could be removed. With pancreatic cancer still inside the body despite the Whipple procedure, the odds remained dismal. Ride's recovery from surgery was "grueling," and, within a couple of months, she had lost a lot of weight and wasn't eating much. After the cancer spread to her bones, Ride underwent additional chemotherapy treatment as well and then radiation, too. By July, "Sally was failing fast."[15]

Cancer progression involves a process in which the body—the person—fails to thrive.

My mother was failing fast too at that time, though it's often difficult to track accurately someone's demise from up close as it's happening. It's also difficult to know whether the inability to eat, the nausea, and the diarrhea worsen more from the progression of the disease or from the side effects of the treatment.

Because my mother's tumor was likely to irritate nerves nearby as it grew larger and because she had known someone

FIGURE 1.2 Brigid (author's sister), Mary Lee (author's mother), and Anna Leahy (author) in hospital room. Hats worn for the Kentucky Derby. Note the sign indicating the patient should have no cold beverage or food for five days because of side effects of chemotherapy.

else who'd suffered severe pain as pancreatic cancer progressed, my mother opted to undergo six chemotherapy treatments in an attempt to keep the tumor as small as possible for as long as possible and to put off the use of opioids to which she was allergic. She had no illusions that this treatment would cure her and would not have opted for it solely to extend her life. Chemo—anti-cancer drugs—was administered intravenously and left my mother with a host of side effects, some of which, in hindsight or if we'd been able to see the forest for the trees, might (perhaps should) have led her to stop chemo before the last treatment or two. She chose this option in hopes it would decrease the length and severity of pain at the end of her life, which it likely did. This stopgap undoubtedly also gave her a few extra months of life.

Even so, my mother died on December 12, 2012, slightly longer than nine months after she was diagnosed.

Father

In October 1981, my father felt ill during our family trip to Ireland and, upon arriving back in the Unites States, drove straight from the airport to his general practitioner. After undergoing several medical tests, he was diagnosed with metastasized liver cancer. But during the exploratory surgery, which revealed tiny blister-like tumors of liver cancer on the lining of his abdomen and the outside of abdominal organs, the surgeon could not locate a primary tumor. Unexpectedly, there was no discernible site where the cancer had begun.

The surgeon and the oncologist told my mother that my father would likely live between two and six weeks. He was forty-eight years old, with two daughters in high school. The oncologist suggested throwing chemotherapy at the problem to see whether that could extend my father's life. Though he'd asked for the treatment to be scheduled the next day so as to decouple the event from other life milestones, my father started chemotherapy on my sixteenth birthday.

Two years later, my father was still alive, and I left for college two hours away, close enough to return quickly if his illness took a turn for the worse. That fall, along with all first-year students at Knox College, I read Leo Tolstoy's novella *The Death of Ivan Ilyich*.[16] Though the ailment wasn't named, the main character, a lawyer like my father, likely suffered from the same cancer as my father or perhaps from the one my mother later suffered. While it might have been some other ailment, the symptoms, the character's physical decline, and the guesswork of treatment were familiar to me. Ivan Ilyich's daughter and I were the same age when our fathers became ill, and our parents had been married the same length of time. That fictional story conveys some long-standing truths about the physical demise and emotional turmoil of an individual in the throes of terminal disease. At the time, though, I only half-recognized what that story was telling me about my own father, the course of terminal illness generally, and the ways in which an individual and the culture respond to such situations.

In an article in the *International Journal of Critical Illness and Injury Science,* Thomas J. Papadimos and Stanislaw P. A. Stawicki discuss the relevance of Tolstoy's fictional story to current-day medical practices and patient care, including the need for "recognition of the dying patient . . . because only about half of dying patients realize that they are actually dying."[17] Fully disclosing to the patient his own situation may seem an obvious necessity, especially to those of us in the United States or Northern Europe. While sometimes some family members or even a physician perceive keeping the cancer diagnosis and/or the prognosis from the patient as beneficial to the patient's well-being, the United States has a strong tradition of patient autonomy, and legal consent for treatment requires that a patient be informed about the risks of a medical intervention. Logically, the patient would need to know the diagnosis and possibly the prognosis in order to decide whether the risks of a particular treatment are worth it, especially for treatment such as surgery, chemotherapy, or radiation.

In some cultures, such as in areas of Japan and China, however, the role of the family or physician supersedes patient autonomy. Sometimes, for instance in some heavily Catholic communities in regions of South America, cancer is thought to be punishment or destiny.[18] In these environs, keeping the diagnosis from the patient, perhaps using vague language to describe what cannot be ignored as illness, may be defined not only as a family member's right but also a responsibility. What son or daughter would want to bring anxiety, despair, or shunning upon a parent? Besides, if the physician is the most knowledgeable on the subject of disease, why not let the doctor decide? Moreover, a study conducted in Iran in 2009 indicated that half the patients did not know their cancer diagnosis and concluded that those patients were better off for their obliviousness.[19] Might the patient who doesn't know that he has cancer be happier, even as he faces treatment for the cancer he doesn't know he has? On the other hand, a study in India, where the physician often informs the family first and the family may request that diagnosis be withheld from the patient, revealed that cancer patients who knew their diagnosis "exhibited a strong need for information about illness and treatment."[20] Is knowledge power in the face of a tumor?

My father was informed of his diagnosis, and he actively participated in the decision-making over the five years of cancer care. He knew his situation was dire, but he probably did not know that he was likely to die within a few weeks. He was not told that first prognosis of two to six weeks, and, in 1981, no one could scour the internet for cancer statistics.

The researchers who discussed the relevance of *The Death of Ivan Ilyich* to today's medical practices pointed to it as revelatory regarding the lack of ability physicians have in predicting outcomes, the under treatment of pain, and the emotional ranges of despair and of empathy among all involved. Physicians guess, don't take pain as seriously as they might, and often don't adjust how they convey information for more or less emotional or more or less knowledgeable patients. If physicians are not particularly good at predicting outcomes, why share a detailed prognosis? If physicians are not well equipped to exhibit their own empathy nor to address the range of a patient and family's emotional needs, would my father's knowledge of a more specific outcome have helped him make more informed decisions, or would that ticking clock of guesswork have clouded his ability to think clearly about his own needs and wants?

This poignant connection between a hundred-year-old literary text and the real-life practice of medicine today is discussed also by surgeon Atul Gawande in his bestselling *Being Mortal,* where he notes, "As we medical students saw it, the failure of those around Ivan Ilyich to offer comfort or to acknowledge what is happening to him was a failure of character and culture. . . . We were confident that in such a situation we would act compassionately. . . . So we put Ivan Ilyich out of our heads."[21] A few years later, as a practicing surgeon, he realized how much this tale revealed and how unprepared he was to act compassionately, in addition to knowledgably, when dealing with a patient confronting mortality.

In the second season of the television show *Scrubs,* Dr. Perry Cox and Dr. Christopher Turk peer from the hospital's hallway into a room in which a patient has died. Though the viewer cannot hear what the physician is telling the patient's family, Dr. Cox explains to Turk, "He's going to tell them what happened, and then he's going to say that he's sorry. And then he's going back to work." The physician has no time to grieve, for the next patient is waiting for his attention. "You think anybody else in that room is going back to work today?

That is why we distance ourselves. That's why we make jokes. We don't do it because it's fun. We do it so we can get by."[22] Everyone involved in a cancer diagnosis must figure out how to get by, but each role makes different demands on the individual.

Indeed, what is the best response by the physician, the patient, family, friends, and co-workers to cancer and to what playwright Eve Ensler called "this chemo forest of claustrophobic annihilation, violent puking, six treatments, numbness, infection, death"?[23] While it's difficult to separate symptoms of the disease from side effects of the treatment, those early rounds of chemo were brutal, leaving my father half his weight, unable to lift his arms overhead, and bald. He looked as if he'd aged thirty years. As columnist Christopher Hitchens wrote about his own treatment for esophageal cancer, "It's quite something, this chemo-poison. It has caused me to lose about fourteen pounds, though without making me feel any lighter."[24] Diminishing the cancer leaves the patient diminished. The chemo worked for my father, not to cure the cancer but to roll back the clock. My father was able to come home from the hospital after three months, on what he understood as borrowed time and in a beleaguered body.

Liver cancer is extremely rare in the United States, with a 9 percent lifetime risk,[25] and it was even rarer thirty years ago. My father's physicians talked about everything they were doing to treat him as if it were experimental. They had never seen a case like his and wondered why in the world he had developed such a rare cancer at such a young age. After going over my father's history, they determined that the likely cause was his military service in the 1950s.

Risk factors are tricky. More men than women develop liver cancer, so being male puts a person at greater risk for liver cancer than being female, but very few men ever get the disease. Chronic hepatitis B or hepatitis C infection is a risk factor, but a vaccine for the former has been available since the 1970s, and the latter is treatable. Cirrhosis, damage to the liver that results in inflammation and thickening of the tissue, is another risk factor and can be caused by high alcohol consumption in addition to hepatitis B or hepatitis C infection. Diabetes 2 is a risk factor, but usually in combination with other risk factors, such as obesity, heavy drinking, or hepatitis infection. Because the liver filters blood and helps rid the body of toxic substances, it makes sense that exposure to certain toxic substances, like cigarette smoke, arsenic, or anabolic steroids, puts a person at greater risk for this cancer. It's difficult, however, to tease apart risk factors or to determine which correlations are actually causes of cancer in a particular individual. Some people diagnosed with a particular cancer live with none of its identified risk factors. None of the usual risk factors known now explained why a man in his forties, who didn't smoke and whose liver was otherwise in good shape, would develop liver cancer.

Thirty years before he was diagnosed, my father was drafted into the US Army and did most of his requisite two-year stint at a weapons depot in Germany. After determining that enough time had passed that he could reveal his classified work there, he described his job as scraping corrosion off nuclear warheads that had been brought back from the border for maintenance and repair.[26] He wore a dosimeter badge on his uniform when he did this work. The badge contained film to measure exposure to ionizing radiation. Ionizing radiation is a known risk factor for several types of cancer. My father remembered tossing the badge into a bin with all the other men's dosimeters so that the Army could track their exposure, but he was never told what the readings were and wondered whether anyone actually recorded any of it.

Once my father was diagnosed with cancer, my mother sought out his military records, but they had burned in a fire on one floor of the storage facility in St. Louis. Eighty percent of the Army's personnel records between 1912 and 1960 were destroyed.[27] The Radiation Exposure Compensation Program includes liver cancer as one of many compensable diseases, diseases known to be caused by exposure to radiation and, therefore, listed specifically in the policy as covered by the program. But the policy covers only veterans directly involved in above-ground nuclear weapons testing, civilians in the path of fallout from that testing, and uranium miners.[28] It did not apply to my father, nor did it apply to veterans exposed in Hiroshima or Nagasaki in the aftermath of the atomic bombings at the end of the Second World War. Without his military personnel record, my father couldn't establish that he'd been involved in work that exposed him to radiation known to cause the particular type of cancer he developed. When my mother was trying to find his military records, the law that compensated veterans didn't exist. Of course, determining the cause of a person's cancer after he's been diagnosed with it doesn't help prevent it in the first place, and not all cancers can be prevented.

When tumor markers—high levels of certain proteins—in my father's blood took an upswing, his oncologist suggested more chemotherapy. Even though greater amounts and more frequent use of some anti-cancer drugs increase the risks, including damage to the heart,[29] my father opted for more 5-FU. Eff you, indeed.

If it had worked before, he thought, maybe it would work again, and what did he have to lose? This time, though, my father wore a continuous infusion pump on his waistband to spread the dosage out over time and, thereby, minimize side effects. A tube ran from the pump up to the catheter—another thin tube—in his chest and delivered chemo drugs into his body for days and weeks at a time. In his oncologist's infusion suite, he'd gather regularly with a group of patients undergoing similar treatment to get his pump checked and refilled. Sometimes, someone would be missing, perhaps hospitalized; one time, two of the group had died between gatherings.

Eventually, even though this treatment had slowed the proliferating cancer, his cancer markers kept climbing, his heart had trouble keeping up with even his diminished body's meager demands, and he was wasting away. That's a word from the death certificate: *wasting*. The cancer and its treatment combined to fell him. Just as when he was diagnosed, my father spent three months in the hospital at the end of his life. He died on July 20, 1986, not quite five years after he was diagnosed. The five-year survival rate for liver cancer overall, even now three decades later with some advances in treatment options, is 17.5 percent and in the wee percentage points for the sort of metastasis with which my father was first diagnosed.[30] He definitely beat the odds, and he died anyway.

Because his case was so unusual, especially for the time, his physicians asked my mother to approve an autopsy for research purposes. Even then, no primary—or original—tumor could be found. Cancer begins with a tumor, except when it doesn't.

Me

In the fall of 2014, a three-dimensional digital mammogram—a fancy x-ray photograph of the breast—showed a few microcalcifications. Calcifications are usually harmless deposits that appear as tiny white spots on a mammogram and that may come and go. Most microcalcifications are benign, but some are an early sign that breast cancer might be developing. Six months later, I returned for a follow-up mammogram to see whether the number of calcifications had changed. Indeed, there were many more.

The radiologist who read the mammogram recommended a core needle biopsy, which uses, as the name suggests, a large needle to extract tissue so that it can be analyzed. The biopsy revealed a small area of atypical lobular hyperplasia. Hyperplasia is an overgrowth of cells—in this case the cells of the milk glands (lobular)—and these proliferating cells, like cancer, were not typical. These misaligned, odd-looking cells were a thickening, not exactly an overgrowth. I did not have a tumor, and I did not have cancer.

Still, my general practitioner, the surgeon I saw, and an oncologist I consulted informally all agreed that this area of abnormal growth should be removed surgically. It could become a cancerous tumor in the future, and it significantly raised my risk of developing breast cancer, whether or not it was removed.[31] So, even though I did not have a tumor or cancer, I underwent a lumpectomy, the same surgical procedure my mother had undergone for her breast cancer. More than a year later, it's difficult to tell anything at all was removed. The area of atypia was so small that its absence didn't affect the size or shape of the breast, and the scar was placed purposefully discreetly and healed well. All's well that ends well. All's well that may not have been the start of anything at all.

I also opted for genetic testing to see whether I had inherited specific genetic mutations that might make me more likely to get cancer. My mother's post-menopausal bout with breast cancer wasn't too disconcerting, as hereditary breast cancer is more likely to strike young. Most women who develop breast cancer have no genetic predisposition or strong family history of the disease. But ovarian cancer cells had been found when an aunt had a hysterectomy for unrelated medical reasons before she had turned fifty (she's still thriving in her seventies), and some genetic mutations associated with breast cancer are also associated with ovarian cancer. There exist at least ten known mutations that link these two cancers and can be passed down in families through the genes. The most well known of these mutations are *BRCA1* and *BRCA2*, either of which significantly increases one's risk for breast cancer, ovarian cancer, and, as more recently discovered, pancreatic cancer.[32]

Even more concerning to the genetic counselor was that my father had developed liver cancer before he turned fifty, combined with the fact that his mother had developed colon cancer in her forties and then died of brain cancer a couple of decades later. In addition, his brother had developed gallbladder cancer (though in his eighties), and his maternal aunt had died of bladder cancer (though in her nineties). That each family member with cancer had a different type is usually a good thing, making it less likely that the family shares a particular genetic mutation. Lynch syndrome, however, is a genetic condition that predisposes a person to all of these cancers on my father's side of the family. If I had a known genetic mutation for Lynch syndrome, that would warrant increased regular screening, including more frequent colonoscopy starting at a younger age than is usually recommended for the general population. My insurance approved genetic testing based on the family history of breast and ovarian cancer, and I chose a set of tests that included looking for genetic mutations related

Lynch Syndrome Pedigree

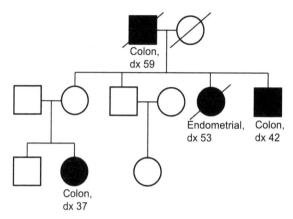

FIGURE 1.3 A simple example of an individual's cancer pedigree or lineage. A square represents male; a circle represents female. Those affected by cancer are filled in or darkened; dx indicates a cancer diagnosis and is followed by age at diagnosis. Those who are deceased are marked with a diagonal line. Source: National Cancer Institute.

to Lynch syndrome as well. The news for me was good. The analysis showed none of the mutations from the list. My genes appeared perfectly normal.

That's not to say that I won't end up with one of these cancers or some other type of tumor. Just because no genetic mutation is found doesn't mean that cancer doesn't run in a family. Pancreatic cancer can run in families, for various possible reasons and combinations of nature and nurture, even when no genetic mutation is pinpointed. Breast cancer, too, can run in families, even when no genetic warning light has gone off. Importantly, the vast majority women who develop breast cancer do not have a family member who's had the disease, and even fewer of those who develop pancreatic cancer have a family member who's had it. Cancer generally or of a particular kind is not all that simply predicted. No person can look at his family or at her own genes and know whether or not he or she will get cancer.

That's the way the math of cancer works. In his book *The Cancer Chronicles,* George Johnson writes, "You could live your life with a calculator. . . . When you're healthy and cancer remains an abstraction, enumerating life's hazards can be reassuring."[33] We'd like to be comforted when statistics seem to point to someone else, when risk factors don't indict our own habits or environment, and when the pristine results of genetic testing are laid before us like get-out-of-jail-free cards. If the average height of the American male is 5' 9",[34] how tall will the next man who walks through the door be? One of two men and one of three women are diagnosed with cancer at some point in their lives, but which one of three? Will it be me?

Based on my own medical history, my mother's history of breast cancer, and my age, my statistical risk of breast cancer is now roughly one in three, almost three times that of the average American woman. Based on this estimated risk, I now alternate mammogram and MRI every six months to screen for breast cancer. I've been prescribed an oral breast cancer prevention drug for post-menopausal women that might lower that risk by fifty percent. And I've hit the age at which colonoscopy is recommended every ten years to screen for colorectal cancer.

To live one's life with a calculator: The word *calculus* originally referred to a pebble—a lump—used for counting. Half of men and one-third of women will develop invasive cancer. Two of my two parents developed malignant tumors; they both took their lumps. I am older than my father was when he was diagnosed; my mother lived two decades longer than I have lived thus far. Cancer math is rough reckoning, an attempt to settle one's account in life, a story of numbers as well as a story of tumors that we tell ourselves.

I am waiting for my tumor. I am waiting to find out which cancer might befall me. I am waiting to see whether I'll get through life without ever having a tumor of my own at all.

2 TERMS AND CONDITIONS

What's in a name?

In the famous window scene of Shakespeare's *Romeo and Juliet*, the two lovers are concerned about the rivalry between their families that threatens to keep them apart. Optimistic Juliet ponders, "What's in a name? that which we call a rose / By any other name would smell as sweet."[1] She suggests that Romeo doff his name, as if his name is the real problem, even as she admits that he'll be the same guy she loves no matter his name. The term used to describe a condition is and is not the condition. A rose is a rose. A tumor is a tumor.

It's not easy to separate the thing itself from the term we use to identify the thing. Moreover, the terms we assign to things shape the larger ways we talk about them and, on a deeper level, the ways we think about and react to them. One out of every two men and one of every three women will be diagnosed with cancer,[2] yet few people think about what a tumor really is or means until we know someone with a tumor or have one of our own. Many of us, only then, will eventually need to figure out what a tumor means and what it means to have a tumor. In her memoir-meets-sociology, S. Lochlann Jain writes, after her diagnosis and first surgery, "Cancer, in all its nounishness, refers to everything . . . and nothing."[3] Her tumor removed, her experience of cancer was still beginning.

The word *cancer*, of course, can mean several things. It's the Latin word for *crab* that refers to the fourth sign of the zodiac and to those born under this sun sign in late June through late July. Depending on whom you ask, a Cancer is thought to be loyal, strong willed, or emotive, qualities that could be applied to the medical meaning of cancer as well, in its affinity for the body in which it emerges, in its tenaciousness, and in its ability to wreak emotional havoc despite its lack of sentience. SpaceX and Tesla entrepreneur Elon Musk, Academy Award-winning actor Tom Hanks, prescient writer George Orwell, and Diana, Princess of Wales—all Cancers. Nothing more than happenstance links them, just as happenstance is the strongest link (that isn't a link) among instances of cancer. In an essay about his experience as a patient in a hospital in 1929, Orwell sees a man who has died of cirrhosis (or possibly cancer) of the liver and poses the question, "What weapon has man invented that even approaches in cruelty some of the commoner diseases?"[4]

The zodiac sign from ancient times is named for the faint constellation that, in the Northern Hemisphere, is best viewed in March. While fuzzy to the naked eye, its Beehive cluster of stars was first studied by astronomer Galileo Galilei in 1609 with a telescope he made himself, was included in Charles Messier's catalog of astronomical objects in 1769, and can be seen as individual twinkles with binoculars today. While the constellation is associated with the crab, this star formation doesn't look particularly crab-like, and the Greek myth in which Hera placed a crab in the sky isn't much about the stomped-upon crustacean. And yet, the word *cancer* has been mapped across the stars and embedded in a story.

Hippocrates, the Greek who likely wrote the oath for physicians that has been adapted to modern times as a promise to do no harm, first called a mass of malignant cells *karkinos* in about 400 BC. It's not clear why he thought *crab* when he looked at a tumor. Maybe it was hard like a crab's shell, or maybe he'd used pincers, like a crab's claw, to pluck it out of the patient's body. A Roman philosopher seems to have later translated that term into the Latin word for crab: *cancer*. The ancient term *karkinos* still lingers, too, in the contemporary use of *carcinoma*, which refers to a cancer whose origins are in epithelial cells that line the body's surfaces (including its ducts and glands) inside and out. Cancers of the breast, lungs, liver, pancreas, and colon are almost always carcinomas, tumors that first arise from the epithelial cells of those organs.

Cancer is singular, yet the disease is multiple. There are more than a hundred types of cancer, and each instance and experience of cancer is individual. Even now, thousands of years after an overgrowth mass of odd cells was first named, Jain points out in *Malignant: How Cancer Becomes Us*, "The word's tangibility dissolves in sheer bafflement, for doctors and patients alike, over what, exactly, it describes."[5]

At least a tumor is an object and, therefore, less baffling than the abstraction or multiplicity of cancer. Sometimes, a tumor can be felt under the skin; a patient might finger its size and shape and allow a physician to palpate it as well. Sometimes, a tumor can be seen on an x-ray; through an MRI, or magnetic resonance imaging, that uses magnets and radio waves to map the body's water and fat; or via an ultrasound in which the echoes of sound waves at higher frequencies than humans can hear are turned into visual images. The shadow that is the image of a tumor is a dot, a splotch, or a burst of light in the darkness of the human-body background portrayed on the screen. Anything that is solid—bone, heart, tumor—becomes a shade of white against the blackish background of the body as universe.

The word *tumor* comes from the Latin for *swelling*. Indeed, a tumor is an overgrowth, a mass of tissue too large or unseemly for the body's own good. Cells proliferate wildly and clump into something that doesn't belong. The medical term for such a thing inside the body is *neoplasm,* which comes from words meaning *new growth*. A tumor is not necessarily cancer, and cancer is not necessarily a tumor. A tumor is new and different. Sometimes, it seems all the same, only more—much more—but the unfamiliar, the previously untraveled, makes all the difference.

In 2012, CNN reported the removal of a noncancerous tumor from the leg of a man in Vietnam; the tumor had been growing since Nguyen Duy Hai was four years old and, at one hundred eighty pounds, weighed twice as much as the man did.[6] In 2009, in a peer-reviewed medical journal, two physicians reported the removal of a fifty-pound ovarian tumor, relatively harmless except for its size and weight; the patient had noticed abdominal swelling two years earlier and had become unable to eat or walk because of the tumor's enormity.[7] Extremely large tumors are extremely rare, but tabloids occasionally run stories about the removal of supposed hundred-pound or even three-hundred-pound tumors that got carried away with themselves. No ordinary swelling, the ability of a tumor to keep growing and growing fascinates us. In a more-is-better world, relatively harmless tumors are just too much, and we don't understand. These enormous, oddball tumors are all the more intriguing because they do not foretell the death that cancer might.

Even tiny lumps in a breast can throw our minds and lives for a loop because we associate tumors with cancer. But not all tumors are cancerous, and not all lumps are tumors. A mole is a tumor, but it's just a mole—unless or until maybe it's not just a mole. A lump in the breast may be a fluid-filled cyst that waxes and wanes as hormones rise and fall or a fibroadenoma, which is a tumor that often feels like a smooth rubber marble under the skin. *Oma* is, in fact, the Latinate medical term for a tumor. A fibroadenoma is a mass of connective (fibro-) and glandular (adeno-) tissue that usually poses no threat to one's health. Carcinoma, sarcoma, or blastoma, however, are terms for types of cancers based on the types of cells that started overgrowing in the first place. Beware the oma that is not kindly and caring, that bodes a bad day.

Benign comes from Latin words meaning *well born*—anyone who has a tumor hopes that it's of the well-born variety. Something benign poses no threat. Sticks and stones may break your bones, but something benign will never hurt you. To be benign is to be gentle and compassionate, like the oma that is your German grandmother. The benign may go unnoticed. Benign? Whatever. The benign is ineffectual.

A benign tumor does not spread in distant places, nor does it usually invade surrounding tissue. It is what it is and stays where it is. A benign tumor may continue to grow, however, and can crowd nearby organs and pinch blood vessels. The greater the size and proximity to vital organs, the more deleterious the mass effect of an otherwise harmless tumor can be. But its growth is usually slow, which might explain how the Indian woman with the fifty-pound ovarian cyst, but with no other or overwhelming symptoms of ill-health, had grown used to the unusual object inside her over months, until, unable to get around on her own while carrying the extra mass, she finally decided to do something about it. Some types of tumors produce hormones, such as insulin or cortisol, that can be harmful, but most tumors are what they are and need not be treated unless or until additional symptoms impede the goings-on in a patient's life.

An exception to the relative harmlessness of benign tumors is the desmoid tumor, which occurs in the connective tissue that supports bones and muscles. It's a rare condition, with only nine hundred people diagnosed per year in the United States, making accurate statistical information hard to come by.[8] Because a desmoid tumor can't spread to distant parts of the body, it's considered benign. That said, it can invade surrounding tissue, and desmoid tumors can recur even after they've been removed surgically. The treatment options are surgery, chemotherapy, and radiation, along with medication to control symptoms like pain and inflammation. In many respects, a desmoid tumor may as well be cancer and is often treated as such. A rose that's not a rose?

In addition, a desmoid tumor may point to familial adenomatous polyposis, an inherited condition that leads to the growth of hundreds, sometimes thousands, of polyps—tiny growths on the mucous lining—in the intestine and, if left untreated, to colon cancer. For those with this condition, a genetic mutation in tumor suppressor genes inhibits the body's usual responses to aging cells. In other words, the genetic mutation doesn't cause cancer directly but makes it tough for the body to nip a potentially cancerous colon cell in the bud or keep a desmoid tumor from developing in the abdomen, shoulder, or leg. It's not the tumor's fault for growing; it's the body's fault for not stopping its growth. The body's not purposefully making a mess, but it's as if the body's stopped doing regular, thorough housecleaning.

Malignant, if one goes back far enough, comes from Latin words meaning *badly born*. A tumor is born—and borne—either well or badly. The Latin *malignantem* means *scheming maliciously,* as if cancer is intentionally plotting against us. In the sixteenth century, that Latin participle came to be applied to the Catholic Church by Protestant writers; the *ecclesiam malignantem* were supposed followers of the antichrist.[9] A tumor, of course, has no agency or intent, no malice toward a particular organ or individual. Yet when told one has a malignancy—a cancer—one may think that tumor is a devious, even unholy, thing. Literary scholar Susan Gubar writes, "I felt that my body had been betrayed or had betrayed me, but I could not comprehend why or when or exactly how a malevolent presence had trespassed into the core of my being."[10] Malignant tumors have trespassed against us; they are out to get us. As Mukherjee notes about this king of all diseases, "The image—of cancer as our desperate, malevolent, contemporary doppelgänger—is so haunting because it is at least partly true."[11]

All the world's a stage

In Shakespeare's play *As You Like It,* one of the characters offers the following insight: "All the world's a stage, / And all the men and women merely players; / They have their exits and their entrances, / And one man in his time plays many parts."[12] One day, a person is playing the part of an attorney running her own law firm, and the next day, that person dons a hospital gown, relinquishes her flesh, and weighs her options on the scales of the injustice that is cancer. Her exit may be coming sooner than she'd expected when she was first learning her lines. She has more to say and had hoped for another scene.

Just as the world is a stage for the individual person, the body is a stage upon which the happenstance of a tumor plays out. The word *stage* comes from the Latin for *stand* or *set,* and the tumor sets itself in place and takes its mark—makes its mark—inside the body. When it comes to malignant tumors, a stage is not only the platform upon which illness performs but also the step or phase in the process of the tumor's development. Cancer is staged.

Stage 0. Cancer in this phase of development is barely cancer at all. It's the iffy whiff of abnormalcy that portends maliciousness, but it's not going anywhere. One just doesn't know whether anything will come of it. Yet the discerning radiologist can find it with increasingly sophisticated imaging of some body parts, and what we find is named and, if at all possible, treated. If we cannot name and treat something, we tend not to look for it.

Sometimes, this numerical label leads to waiting and watching; other times, to surgical removal. In fact, in some cases, the biopsy to confirm a diagnosis will remove the entirety of the problem. We treat it not because of what it is but because of what it might—or might not—become. Stage 0 is the exceptional phase at which treatment can lead relatively quickly to cure, a word that physicians usually avoid when discussing cancer even as they are actively treating it. Rarely is a patient told she is cured, only that she is cancer free.

Not all cancers can be detected at this stage of development, however. The number zero describes ductal carcinoma in situ—Stage 0 breast cancer—or just-barely-cancer of the skin, lung, cervix, or uterus. There is not yet a meaningful almost-there or just-turned-the-corner for pancreatic cancer, lymphoma, or many others. Certainly, this stage might exist for any cancer, but a stage is only as good as the ability to view it from the best seats in the house, test for it with relative accuracy, and treat it.

Stage I. So attached is medicine to its Latin origins of terminology that phases of cancer development are often enumerated in Roman, instead of the commonly used Arabic, numbers. Stage I describes a localized tumor, one that hasn't invaded surrounding tissues nor sent its malignant cells to nearby lymph nodes or other parts of the body.

But staging has become more nuanced than that. Stages can be parsed even further. Stage IA breast cancer describes a tumor smaller than two centimeters with no lymph node involvement, but Stage IB refers to a small tumor with spots in one to three underarm lymph nodes, though each spot there must be no greater than two hundred cells or two millimeters, lest the diagnosis slip into Stage II.[13] Even though the breast cancer has spread to the lymph nodes this parsing suggests that Stage IB acts and can be addressed more like Stage IA than like Stage II.

Stage II. Depending on the type of cancer, Stage II is generally assigned because the tumor has grown beyond the size designated for Stage I. Or the tumor has invaded surrounding tissue, or both. Malicious cells may have spread to the lymph nodes with intent to do damage elsewhere, but no evil elsewhere is detected. Everything's still relatively local.

The possibilities for Stage II and Stage III breast cancer can be parsed into several combinations of tumor size and lymph node involvement, with designations of A and B like an outline for one's first high-school research paper based on what one knows and thinks will pan out in order to at least pass the course, if not excel in knowing exactly what to do next. For pancreatic cancer, Stage I and Stage II are parsed further with A and B versions, based on tumor size and whether cancer has spread to nearby lymph nodes, but there's no need to separate versions of Stage III, for any distinctions have no useful meaning for decision-making or prognosis when it comes to pancreatic cancer. What's done is done.

Stage III. Stage III, as expected, is direr than Stage II. The tumor has invaded lymph nodes and/or blood vessels. *Progression* means *to move forward*, and Stage III means that the tumor has been plodding along, waiting to unleash itself. The disease has progressed; the disease is progressed. It's on its way to other body parts, but it's not there yet.

While she doesn't talk about staging in a clinical sense, Carla Malden writes about the initial diagnosis of her husband's colon cancer in ways that capture what a cancer stage means to a patient and his family: "Everything that happened in the next few hours amounted to a good news/

bad news tug-of-war. Lymph node involvement—yes. Liver involvement—no. I cried either way, whatever the news."[14] Eve Ensler talks about staging of ovarian cancer in a more clinical sense in her memoir: "The Mayo team, being more literal, determined me to be IVB (there was cancer in my lymph nodes in my groin). Beth Israel was seeing me as IIIB. Either way, it was all Bs again. All bad."[15] All bad, and not as clear-cut as one might think when a confident physician in a white coat delivers the diagnosis. Oh, to be number one! Oh, to earn the A, whenever the B looms as a possibility.

Stage IV. Cancer does not go to eleven. No re-dividing of the cancer dial will lead to anything louder than Stage IV. Renumbering, like Nigel Tufnel's assertions about his amplifier in the film *Spinal Tap,* would be a matter of semantics over the same range of disease progression. At Stage IV, even if it were to be given another name, the cancer would still be as bad. A tumor is a tumor; a stage is a stage.

At Stage IV, cancer has already spread to distant parts of the body. Breast cancer, if it metastasizes, may spread almost anywhere, perhaps to the bones, the liver, or the lungs. There's not much parsing of this phase to do, though lung cancer can be separated into Stage IVA, in which metastasis remains in the chest area, and Stage IVB, in which the mets or, in UK lingo, secondaries are far off, perhaps in the brain.

The word *metastasis* comes from the Greek meaning *a change or transition* or, going further back, *a shift in position from one place to another.* The former suggests an internal modification or shift in condition, whereas the latter suggests an external move in location or geography. The former, as applied to cancer, offers a way to consider the disease; the latter offers a way to consider cancer as object. By the 1660s, the latter definition was applied as a medical term,[16] especially fitting for late-stage cancer that has moved from one place in the body to another, whether or not it has been surgically removed from its original perch. Metastasis also suggests that the body itself has made a transition, no longer merely having cancer but ridden with it, no longer containing cancer but being overtaken by it. Likewise, there's a change in treatment options and patient care—often to palliative care focused entirely on the relief of symptoms rather than on the elimination of disease—and also a transition in mindset for patient and physician, a movement toward chronic disease or the final reckoning.

There exists no Stage V. Metastasis is the end-all of the be-all.

Cancer is assigned its stage at diagnosis, and there's no going backward or forward. If a woman diagnosed with Stage II breast cancer later develops metastasis or secondary tumor sites, it may feel and be treated as if it were Stage IV, but it is still called, in the bookkeeping, Stage II with metastasis. Laurence, Malden's husband, underwent surgery and chemotherapy. Then, "The second go-round blindsided us almost as much as the first, if that is possible."[17] His diagnosis had been Stage III, but the cancer had spread. He had "three tiny nodules in the peritoneal cavity" and "a coating around the liver."[18] The couple clung to the fact that the cancer had not invaded the liver itself, but metastasis is metastasis. It may as well have been Stage IV, and, if it hadn't been discovered until then, it would have been diagnosed as such. Medical record keeping defines the disease at diagnosis. Patients are not re-diagnosed but, rather, stripped away toward cancer free or coated over in metastasis, swaying or lurching one way or the other from the initial pivot point of diagnostic staging.

Upon diagnosis, the game's afoot. If the cancer is excised, good riddance. If the cancer progresses, the terminology doesn't catch up so much as it piles on, and the devil that is cancer collects its due. Cancer forces a person to catch up with all her yesterdays, or her yesterdays catch up with her as she realizes that tomorrows may be less likely. Even if treatment is successful, the experience of cancer makes one conscious that no one lives forever and a day, though even the terminal cancer patient often thinks one more day is likely, at least possible.

3 SELF/OTHER(S)

The object that is you

Tumor is the object that is you.

Though they are often excised at the first hint of trouble, as if they are foreign objects, as if one of these things just doesn't belong, tumors are part of the body, are made of the body. Tumors are body.

The body makes cancer cells in the same way that it makes healthy cells. "In a normal cell, powerful genetic circuits regulate cell division and cell death. In a cancer cell, these circuits have been broken, unleashing a cell that cannot stop growing."[1] Whether benign or malignant, the cells of a tumor result from the same process as any other cells. As nineteenth-century scientist Rudolf Virchow noted, the only place a cell can come from is another cell. The process of mitosis creates two identical cells—each with its own, identical set of chromosomes—from one. Cell division is vital for the body to grow and to repair itself. Cell growth is a natural process; cells grow in our bodies all the time.

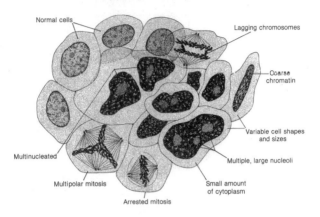

Normal and Cancer Cells

Normal cells

Lagging chromosomes

Coarse chromatin

Variable cell shapes and sizes

Multinucleated

Multiple, large nucleoli

Multipolar mitosis

Small amount of cytoplasm

Arrested mitosis

FIGURE 3.1 Normal and cancer cells shown side by side, with normal and cancer characteristics identified.
Source: National Cancer Institute.

Cell growth is a good and necessary process without which we cannot live. An embryo cannot become a fully formed human being without rapid cell reproduction. The adult body replaces billions of its cells every day. While brain cells last an entire lifetime, colon cells last a few days. Muscles or fat usually grow as cells enlarge, not by adding cell upon cell but by bulking up the cells already present. Organs, however, usually get bigger through hyperplasia, by adding more cells. To increase the number of cells, existing cells divide and divide again. All cells of a human body are descendants of the initial egg and sperm.

Because these natural processes of maturity and expansion are with and in us, the potential for tumors—for awkward growth, for overgrowth—are with and in us as well. Even ancient dinosaurs developed tumors, so these swellings are not particular to humans or to our time, but, rather, a chance any living creature takes in the course of day-to-day-to-year-to-year life. In discussing the long history of cancer, George Johnson writes, "There is something comforting about knowing that cancer has always been with us, that it is not our fault, that you can take every precaution and still something in the genetic coils can become unsprung."[2] To live—for the body to grow and repair itself—is to invite the possibility of a tumor.

Cell growth sustains us. Except when it is too much growth. Then, it is pathological. *Pathology* comes from the Latin meaning *the study of suffering*. Suffering, in this case, is too much of a good thing. Like a fib, one extra or odd cell might be a harmless test of the truth, a comment with no particular ill will behind it or even the best of intentions. With 37.2 trillion cells in the human body,[3] it's no wonder that, every now and then, one misspeaks, divides off kilter, haphazardly carries a meaningful mutation in one of its genes. What else in your life have you made perfectly 37,200,000,000,000 times? What's the harm in one mistake among all those cells? But lying too much is pathological. Cancer starts with one cellular fib the body tells itself. A tumor is the accumulation of lies told again and again and again, the tissue clinging to those cellular misstatements that should have been repudiated or ignored.

Researchers Bert Vogelstein and Christian Tomasetti were particularly interested in explaining why some types of tissue are more likely to develop tumors than others, even after environmental factors and inherited genetic mutations are ruled out. They determined that the greater the number of stem-cell divisions in a type of tissue, the higher the relative chance that type would develop cancer. They racked this up to "bad luck" and randomness in the cell division process and stated "only a third of the variation in cancer risk among tissues is attributable to environmental factors or inherited predispositions."[4] Environmental factors are things people can change: stop smoking, wear sunscreen, get vaccinated for hepatitis B and human papillomavirus, avoid obesity. Inherited predispositions cannot be changed, but one can be tested for known mutations when one's own medical history and one's family history of cancer warrant such inquiry. This study downplayed these two large categories of risk—environment and genetics—over which individuals have some control or about which people have some knowledge.

The lowest-risk cancers Vogelstein and Tomasetti studied were several osteosarcomas, which also had the lowest number of stem-cell divisions, and the highest-risk cancers they studied were Lynch colorectal, FAP colorectal, and basal cell cancers, which had the highest number of stem-cell divisions.[5] The researchers' conclusion was that, in the cancers they studied—they did not study breast cancer, for instance—two-thirds of the *difference* in risk *between*, say, osteosarcoma of the pelvis and basal cell carcinoma could be explained by the variation in the number of stem-cell divisions and the tissue's tendency to retain mutations and, therefore, not by environmental or inherited risk factors.

They did not say or mean that two-thirds of all cancers were a result of bad luck. But that's what people heard.

On New Year's Day in 2015, Jennifer Couzin-Frankel scooped this story about the cellular underpinnings of cancer in *Science*, "Take the number of cells in an organ, identify what percentage of them are long-lived stem cells, and determine how many times the stem cells divide. With every division, there's a risk of a cancer-causing mutation in a daughter cell."[6] That's a reasonable summation of the necessary process of cell division. But in an attempt to tell a clear, succinct story for general readers, she made further conclusions that were oversimplifications that led to overstatements: "This theory explained two-thirds of all cancers."[7] Other journalists picked up on this simple rendering. It's a widely appealing explanation of cancer because it lets patients off the hook, for a person cannot be blamed for his or her own cell divisions. But it undercuts that many cancers are preventable, that cancer incidence rates can be reduced.

More importantly in regard to interpreting this particular study, that statement fails to account for the research as a *comparison* among statistical cancer rates and not an explanation of cancer itself, either generally or in specific types or instances. The distinction missed in the initial and ensuing articles is that between relative and absolute risk. The absolute risk of a man getting cancer is one in two, but that information does not directly apply to small groups nor indicate whether my husband will develop cancer. Relative risk explores why some people might be more predisposed to cancer or why some cancers might be more prevalent in a population than other cancers are. *Absolute* is *free from* specific conditions, whereas *relative*, as its Latin root suggests, *refers* to something, is contingent, is an interpretation of risk.

The absolute lifetime risk of colorectal cancer (Vogelstein and Tomasetti included this one) is 4.5 percent,[8] and the absolute lifetime risk of developing brain or nervous system cancer (glioblastoma was a form of brain cancer included in the study) is a much lower .6 percent.[9] In other words, the risk of colorectal cancer is 7.5 times as great as the risk of glioblastoma. (Oddly, the higher number for relative risk may make colorectal cancer appear a greater risk than it really is.) This study in question attempts to explain that large *difference* between the likelihood of these (and other) cancers, not the reason a person gets cancer. So, less than two weeks later, Couzin-Frankel grappled admirably to understand the mistakes she'd made and corrected herself: "Some tissues are overtaken by cancer more readily than others, and mutations accumulating in stem cells explained two-thirds of that variability."[10]

Cell growth maintains our bodies and allows us to thrive. Except when it is too many cells at once, as in pathological hyperplasia. The cells lying there, one atop another atop another, become recognizable as a pattern, as an object themselves, as a tumor. Or in the case of leukemia, "cancer in a molten, liquid form."[11] While environmental factors can be changed to reduce risk and while genetic testing can be used to target screening and preventative medical intervention, the human body exists in a state of probability. Those tissues in which stem cells divide in greater number over a lifetime pose the greater chance of hyperplasia that is tumor.

Cell growth is a good and necessary process. Except when a cell mistakes itself for itself, when the body disappoints itself, tricks itself, fails itself or when something—cigarette smoke, asbestos exposure, ionizing radiation, the rays of the sun—trips it up. Cancer is the body stumbling, a weakness.

Or so we'd like to think. "Cancer cells grow faster, adapt better," Mukherjee writes. "They are more perfect versions of ourselves."[12] Cells do what they do, and cancerous versions of cells do what they do even better. Cancer, then, is not only the object that is you, but, even stranger, it is the object that is, by some measures, the best version of yourself.

Versions of you

One type of tumor, the teratoma, is especially us, indistinguishable from us only because it is the right tissue in the wrong place. The tumor consists of normal tissue that is not like the normal tissue in which it is situated. As long as it remains benign, it exhibits none of the usual characteristics of cancer and poses a threat only because of its size and location.

Teratomas growing from germ cells—cells that become eggs and sperm—form in the ovaries or testes, whereas teratomas growing from embryonal cells can be found elsewhere, including the brain or the tongue. A teratoma at the base of the spine is the most common tumor found in newborns. The babies born with tails in the "Small Potatoes" episode of *The X-Files*[13] may have been easily explained as newborns with saccrococcygeal teratomas.

These benign growths (those rare malignant ones are staged as cancer) are thought to emerge as the individual comes into being cell by cell, organ by organ. A small clump of tissue inside a growing embryo mistakenly breaks away and ends up encapsulated where it doesn't belong, in another place just forming. Had it stayed where it should, it would have differentiated into exactly the right cells and tissues needed where they were. Misplaced, it can do no good, but it continues to grow anyway, differentiating into the best version of an embryo it can become on its own. The teratoma is a part of a version of the body before it was a body and becomes as close to a body as it can. It is a partial body, a body part—muscle, fat, bone—out of place.

Not only is the teratoma's tissue unlike its surroundings, it is often a mishmash of tissue. The ovarian teratoma may contain hair, teeth, even a limb, as if the tumor is extra parts or the body parts of someone else inside this someone. A fetus may carry what seems to be a parasitic twin. In 2003, surgeons excised the most human-like teratoma from a Japanese woman; it had a brain, limbs, intestines, an eye, an ear.[14] *Teratoma* comes from the Greek for *monstrous tumor*.

Most teratomas, when discovered, can be excised surgically, since they don't invade surrounding tissue. It's as if this tumor does not consider itself part of the body but, rather, a body in and of itself. Not us, but itself. If the teratoma is malignant or if it cannot be removed surgically, as might be the case in the brain, chemotherapy is used.

These growths are the uncanny valley of tumors, enough like us—with hair and teeth—that the thought creeps us out. To ponder the teratoma is to ponder what constitutes the human body. The conclusion to be drawn is that I am human because I am whole. Yet, how many parts are necessary to be physically human, to be functionally human? How much of myself might be removed—might I lose—and still leave me intact as a person? Clearly, a teratoma is not a person, but by exactly how much is it not?

The Tumor is not you

Several decades ago, it was rare to utter or hear the word *cancer*. When John Wayne unexpectedly revealed in a 1964 press conference that he'd had a lung removed to treat cancer that likely resulted from a six-packs-a-day smoking habit and possibly from exposure to fallout from nuclear weapons testing during the filming of *The Conquerer,* he said in lingo of the day, "I licked the Big C."[15] An editorial in *The Lancet* fifty years later, cheerfully asserts, "No longer is cancer the big 'C.'"[16] Letting go of the spell-it-in-front-of-the-children talk of cancer has taken a long time.

Comedian Gilda Radner recalled of her father's illness in 1958, "Nobody ever said the word *cancer*."[17] Years later, in 1986, her malignant ovarian tumor was discovered, and she was readied for surgery within forty-eight hours. Even then, "I do remember that nobody said the word *cancer*."[18] The language used to talk about cancer reflects the social attitudes toward the disease. Chemotherapy had been a mainstay in treatment for only thirty years by the time Radner faced the disease, and many important chemotherapy developments, including for ovarian cancer, occurred only a decade or so earlier. Why say aloud the name of a disease that still seemed a death sentence?

The word for *tumor* in French is the similar *tumeur*, which, as Grant Rosenberg at the American Library in Paris pointed out to me, is much like *tu meurs*, meaning *you die*.

While not words anyone wants to utter much, *cancer* and *tumor* are part of the social conversation about who we are. Our language adjusts as the medical and social context of the disease changes. "A world where some cancers are becoming chronic, lifelong conditions, requires a shift in our perception of the disease and survivorship," argues *The Lancet*.[19] *The Big C* used to be the whispered euphemism for cancer, but now refers to the recent Showtime comedy-drama television series featuring Laura Linney as a character diagnosed with Stage IV melanoma, a type of skin cancer. Cancer became the subject of and vehicle for public storytelling not possible decades earlier. In fact, in her book *Reading & Writing Cancer*, Susan Gubar goes so far as to claim, "We reside in the midst of the development of the cancer canon."[20] She goes on to explain the emergence of cancer literature as the result of patient empowerment, wider access to medical information, requirements for disclosing diagnosis and treatment options, and the blurring between our public and private lives.[21]

The language we use often dismisses the biological fact that the tumor is part of and made out of one's own body and, instead, positions the body in battle with itself or positions the self in battle with the body, as if cancer is an enemy trespasser. A tumor is rendered an invader, an enemy to be vanquished. Obituary after obituary notes that the individual died after a *battle with cancer,* sometimes a long or protracted battle, sometimes a brave or courageous one.

Battle comes from the Latin meaning *to strike or beat,* adapted long ago to refer generally to the sort of fighting that trained soldiers do and then to individual combat or a specific confrontation in a larger war. This militaristic metaphor is used by physicians and patients, as they battle instances of cancer together, and by policy makers and media, as they discuss the overarching research efforts to understand and eradicate cancer on the larger scale of war.

When President Richard Nixon signed the National Cancer Act in 1971, which bolstered the National Cancer Institute and proliferate research-and-clinical cancer centers nationwide, that policy and research effort to eradicate cancer—or at least drastically reduce the number of deaths that result from the disease—was dubbed the War on Cancer. More recently, President Obama, whose mother died of ovarian cancer at the age of fifty-three, less than a year after her diagnosis, included cancer-related funding in his economic stimulus package of 2009. He was quoted in the media using the ubiquitous war metaphor: "Now is the time to commit ourselves to waging a war against cancer as aggressive as the war cancer wages against us."[22] Cancer is the enemy, cancer has attacked us, and we must fight back with everything we've got.

Radner uses the word *battle* numerous times in her memoir about life with ovarian cancer and thinks of herself as inherently a fighter whose skills come in especially handy once she is diagnosed. She discusses the need for the patient—the patient's need? or society's need for the patient?—"to participate in battling cancer." She more specifically explains, "And if you visualize the cancer cells and see them as evil and visualize them being removed from your body, you are supporting the actual process" of healing through chemotherapy.[23] If a patient does not think of the cancer as evil, does that person thwart healing and somehow give cancer the edge? Is the unwillingness or inability to do battle a deal with the devil?

Christopher Hitchens recognized the widespread use of the battle metaphor when he faced esophageal cancer and was troubled by this language. "People don't have cancer: They are reported to be battling cancer. No well-wisher omits the combative image: You can beat this."[24] With wit, he noted the ubiquity of such language in obituaries that are specific to deaths as a result of cancer and its absence when referring to death from heart disease, even though specific lifestyle choices can be made to combat heart disease. We don't battle against just any mortality; we battle against cancer as if we always have a fighting chance. In reality, Hitchens points out about the experience of chemotherapy, "The image of the ardent soldier or revolutionary is the very last one that will occur to you. You will feel swamped with passivity and impotence: dissolving in powerlessness like a sugar lump in water."[25]

Though he didn't make the connection, one might think of the wicked witch disintegrating when Dorothy throws the bucket of water on her in *The Wizard of Oz*. Hitchens's dissolving sugar cube metaphor for himself might have been, instead, a metaphor for destruction of the tumor via chemotherapy and radiation, a whimpering away as if the tumor might evaporate into thin air. This switching of metaphor works. However, any metaphor becomes problematic because the tumor is the body. Hitchens did not feel the tumor was dissolving so much as he on the whole was becoming diluted, weakened, breaking down into bits and pieces.

Proof of the extraordinary extent to which Americans use the battle metaphor is in the made-up, tongue-in-cheek story of the imaginary Russ Kunkel in *The Onion*. In the spoof obituary, Kunkel "died following a brief, cowardly battle with stomach cancer."[26] Kunkel's imaginary wife recalls that, while most people who face cancer summon courage, Russ gave up, cried incessantly, and asked her to honor his memory by never moving on with her own life after he dies. Imaginary friends of this cowardly cancer victim talk of his negative outlook and, in accordance with Russ's last requests for the funeral, scream, cry, and curse the unfairness of his death. To read this obituary is to be made uncomfortable because the man's reactions to impending death from cancer seem both completely out of character from what we expect of each other and also absolutely reasonable given the circumstances. If one is diagnosed with cancer, aren't despair, fear, and outrage appropriate and reasonable reactions? Kunkel is the sugar lump in water that Hitchens reveals as his own real-life scenario. (That said, Hitchens's act of writing is not the act of someone dissolved.) Yet, a passive, impotent cancer patient who is angry about his or her fate is a far less appealing sight (and site) than a brave, upbeat go-getter who helps those around him deal with the situation with courage and warmth as well.

In what was not a spoof but an obituary penned by the deceased before her death, Emily Phillips wrote, "It pains me to admit it, but apparently, I have passed away. Everyone told me it would happen one day but that's simply not something I wanted to hear, much less experience."[27] Phillips had pancreatic cancer and probably knew of—and didn't like— the odds of survival. Hearing bad news may not lead to utter despair, but that doesn't mean it leads to acceptance either, and Phillips admits both surprise and resistance. She penned her own obituary in hospice and died just twenty-nine days after the diagnosis, so she didn't have much time for acceptance or taking up arms to battle her terminal cancer. Once the news sunk in, maybe she had time for a skirmish or a scuffle. In her writing, after recounting memories of her life, some of them quite sentimental, she sums it all up: "I was born; I blinked; and it was over."[28] She doesn't talk about a battle at all. She requests, in reference to what is often attributed to Dr. Seuss or Gabriel García Márquez, that those who attend her funeral not cry because she's gone but smile because she existed at all. How sweet. Too sweet. So she undercuts that sentiment with instructions to cry a bit because, after all, she's dead.

One can imagine that it would be difficult to write about illness as a battle from the perspective of having lost. People don't like to lose; people don't choose to lose or, generally, expect to lose. Even Phillips, who grappled with the inevitability of her impending death, opened with disbelief that it had actually happened. Because we cannot fathom death—as poet Emily Dickinson suggested, we cannot bring ourselves to stop for death[29]—we have difficulty thinking it possible that we will lose the battle against it. And yet, despite our inability to grasp the fact of death or stop for it, death comes around the corner and stops for us. Moreover, the spoof in The Onion points to one of the problems of the battle metaphor for cancer, namely that Russ's inability to fight valiantly—his willingness to stop for death—contributed to his quick demise. If the battle with cancer is lost, the individual who dies is a loser.

Susan Gubar, whose groundbreaking feminist literary criticism I first read as a graduate student twenty-five years ago, also addresses this notion of the battle and the quandary it presents for the inability or refusal to fight. "Cancer patients dedicated to an epic struggle against their disease reject any 'surrender' to it as an act 'of conspiring' with it."[30] The individual who dies is not only a loser, then, but has actually conspired with the enemy, has, by not fighting hard enough, fought on the side of cancer. To not fight is to fight against oneself, even though the tumor is oneself. Gubar suggests, instead, "that no amount of fighting 'can give you back your life,' that it would be a lie 'to live as though the cancer will never return,' and that therefore it is necessary to find a way out of the proposition that if you are not hopefully battling your own cancer, you are somehow rooting for it."[31] The devil's in the details, and there's no dealing with it.

Is there no way around the battle metaphor? Hitchens writes, "I'm not fighting or battling cancer—it's fighting me."[32] So, even if the patient isn't battling, the battle goes on. The cancer is the aggressor, the invader, the enemy. Better to slash wildly with a butter knife while shaking in one's boots than to not raise any weapon in an attempt to slay the evildoer. Playing dead doesn't work to throw this predator off, even if you feel like death warmed over in the midst of a round of chemotherapy. As the lottery slogan goes, you can't win if you don't play. What the lottery doesn't advertise but what we all know anyway is that, even though some people win, playing doesn't guarantee winning.

Eve Ensler, who first penned *The Vagina Monologues* that have since taken on a life of their own, credits her post-therapy therapist-friend with a way to allay her fears of chemo-poison and "reframe the entire chemo experience" so that "Your job is to welcome the chemo as an empathetic warrior, who is coming in to rescue your innocence by killing the perpetrator who got inside you. You have many bodies; new ones will be born out of this transformational time of love and care."[33] This shift seems as close as possible to transforming the battle metaphor into a healing metaphor, perhaps as a journey into a new self over time, without relinquishing the basic premise of self against enemy that has done you wrong.

A journey implies travel and, metaphorically, transition from one state to another, which certainly can be applied to cancer. If life is a journey, as we often hear it is, might cancer be a bag of rocks—metaphorical tumors—strapped to one's back that the patient attempts to discard one at a time to lighten the load, or that dissolve one by one into sand that blows away in the breeze? And if the load becomes heavier, the rocks growing in number through a process akin to metastasis, might the patient pause to catch her breath and put effort into strengthening her legs to keep walking, one foot in front of the other?

A prognosis is a description of the course the disease is likely to take. The word *course* harks back to the Latin verb meaning *to run*, and disease is said to run its course. The body, too, moves onward through time. The word *journey* comes from the Latin meaning *daily*, which offers this way for the patient to consider her cancer: as what this day brings with it, as what she must now contemplate and carry day by day like pebbles used for calculation.

True colors

To *survive* means *to live above or beyond*, to outlive others, to outlive cancer—survival can be a slow race. Like a dance marathon in the 1930s, with couples dancing until they dropped into sleep, the last one standing takes the prize. In hands-on-car contests, the person who does not give up, who will not let loose the feel of metal under hand, wins the car. A soldier survives a battle. Survival is a measure of stamina under physical duress.

It's often assumed, in a mangled tautology based on Charles Darwin's theory of evolution, that survival is hindsight proof of fitness. I'm reminded of the joke in which two hikers, out in the woods on a brisk Saturday, discuss the possibility of a bear encounter. One hiker says to the other, "What should we do if a bear charges us? Neither of us can outrun a bear." The other hiker replies, "I'll be okay. I need only outrun you." Fitness is relative, but anyone can turn his ankle while fleeing a bear.

Common wisdom, of course, is not to flee a black bear but, instead, to face the bear, spread one's arms, and make loud noises. Do not look like prey. Do not run away from something you cannot outrun. A mother grizzly bear, however, may leave a person alone if he plays dead and poses no threat to her offspring.[34] Fitness has less to do with inherent goodness or strength and less to do with competition than with the ability to adapt to situations. And survival of the fittest has nothing to do with individual people and everything to do with genetic variety among us. Survival, like cancer, can be understood as probability.

To survive, one lives in spite of risk, danger, or adversity, not because of fitness. Though one might survive a bear attack, a person does not survive a pleasant hike in the woods. One cannot survive unless there exists something to measure one's continued existence against. Struggle reveals our true colors, an idea thought to echo Hippocrates, the ancient Greek advocate of clinical medicine who believed each individual embodied four temperaments. One can endure and survive atrocities. Sometimes, cancer is that something by which one can measure one's living.

In the noblest sense, a victim—the opposite of survivor, in this sense of facing an atrocity—is a sacrifice, an offering. A victim is harmed or killed by someone else or something else, not of one's own volition or for one's own good. A victim is sapped of power, duped, cheated. Who will be a cancer survivor? Who will be a cancer victim?

Out of the history of tying yellow ribbons around ole oak trees to symbolize the devotion to and hope for return of a loved one who has served time or served in battle comes the colored ribbon as the symbol of perseverance, hope, and commemoration of survivor and victim alike. The 1949 film

She Wore a Yellow Ribbon, starring then healthy and heavily smoking John Wayne, takes its name from the 1917 song "She Wore a Yellow Ribbon," in which the woman wears the decoration in honor of her soldier far away, in hopes that he will survive and return to her unharmed. The hostages in Iran in 1979 were symbolically welcomed home by yellow ribbons around trees even before their release was secured after more than four hundred days in captivity. President Jimmy Carter called the hostages "*victims* of terrorism and anarchy,"[35] but they survived their ordeal. By 1990, AIDS awareness efforts had adopted the yellow ribbon as an emblem for those battling what was a relatively new, stigmatized, and deadly disease. The yellow ribbon is now a symbol for suicide prevention and for endometriosis as well.

In fact, there exists a ribbon for every cancer occasion. Dark blue? Colon cancer. Orange? Kidney cancer. Green? Liver cancer. Purple? Pancreatic cancer. Black? Melanoma, the type of skin cancer the character in *The Big C* had. Black-and-white zebra stripe? Carcinoid tumors. And every big cancer has an awareness month. September: childhood cancer, gynecological cancer, leukemia, lymphoma, ovarian cancer, thyroid cancer, prostate cancer. November: pancreatic, lung, stomach, and carcinoid cancers, and that's Caregivers Month too. If there's a less prevalent cancer that needs more awareness, August is waiting.

No cancer awareness effort has more successfully deployed its ribbon, color, and month than that for breast cancer. October is pink. October is Breast Cancer Awareness Month. The third

Friday of that month is National Mammography Day, and some mammography centers offer reduced rates for screening all month, an important part of the awareness campaign.

The first Race for the Cure, an educational and fundraising event started by the Susan G. Komen Foundation, was held in Dallas in October 1983. Now more than a hundred of these events occur all year and in various locales, with national and local business sponsorship. In fiscal year 2015, this one project—Race for the Cure—raised $86.4 million, and 81 percent of the foundation's total spending went toward education, research, screening, and treatment.[36] For perspective on the success of the Komen Foundation, just one organization supporting breast cancer awareness and research, that's roughly four times what the Pancreatic Cancer Action Network raised the year before across all its fundraising efforts[37] and more than 170 times what the National Pancreatic Cancer Foundation raised in 2015.[38]

Greater funding for breast cancer education, research, screening, and treatment than for pancreatic cancer makes great sense in that breast cancer has a higher incidence rate than other cancers. In part because more women develop breast cancer, it also kills more women in the United States than all but lung cancer.[39] Advances in breast cancer screening and treatment, therefore, are likely to help more people. On the other hand, cancers with higher mortality rates, like pancreatic cancer, might be worthy of more attention and funding to address the direst situations or work toward decreasing mortality rates across all cancer types. Advances in screening for the deadliest cancers could save a lot of lives. In fact, advances in breast cancer screening, including digital and 3D mammography, and changes in treatment demonstrate part of the story of how mortality rates drop when cancers are detected early and can be removed surgically before metastasis. As yet, there exist no such screening techniques for detecting pancreatic cancer or liver cancer when the tumor is small.

Another way to ponder how funding might be best allocated would be to look at disparities among demographic groups instead of considering cancer type alone. African-Americans, for instance, have higher mortality rates than whites for breast, prostate, stomach, cervical, and lung cancers.[40] That area of research involves both biological underpinnings and also societal substructures that lead to disparities in diagnosis and pain management as well as false assumptions about the physical body. Physician overconfidence and authority likely make cultural bias and dependence on logical fallacy in decision-making all the more crucial for the need to investigate disparities in incidence and in mortality among demographic groups.

Even federal funding through the National Cancer Institute, however, is not necessarily doled out according to these overarching questions about the greatest good for the greatest number, nor with a nod to the tricky balance of quantity of lives and quality of life. Instead, grant proposals for NCI funding are evaluated on scientific merit by scientists, which sounds straightforward but also myopic without explicitly considering which research might best translate into clinical use and patient survival, research that might be considered translational between theory and application. Other considerations include the fluctuation in overall NCI funding available and the total number of proposals, the availability of other funding sources for the particular research, and whether the research is just beginning or is ongoing. Sometimes, proposals that address certain kinds of questions, such as how to predict future malignancy in precancerous lesions or how to predict recurrence, are encouraged. All proposals include statements about the goals, significance, originality, approaches, and budget and are judged upon those contents.[41]

Even though the National Institutes of Health (NCI is one of their institutes) discourages so-called me-too research and even as reviewers consider the likelihood that innovative and focused research will lead to useful results and applications, money seems to follow money. In fiscal year 2013, $559.2 million in NCI funding for breast cancer research outstripped any other cancer. Lung cancer research ranked second in NCI funding with $285.9 million, and pancreatic cancer research was supported with less than one-fifth of that for breast cancer.[42] Though a much smaller pool of funding, the American Cancer Society allocations divide up similarly, with breast cancer research most well funded, followed by lung cancer, and pancreatic cancer funded in an amount less than one-seventh of breast cancer.[43]

NIH applicants are also encouraged not to be "bashful" in bragging about accomplishments and to make sure their research goals "sing and harmonize."[44] The need to sing and harmonize suggests that style and personality matter to funding decisions. If funding determines progress, breast cancer seems to be leading by many measures. It certainly has the most style and personality in its public relations—public awareness—campaign.

Retailers, right along with researchers, have jumped on the popular, money-raising, pink bandwagon for the October celebration. The over-thirty-five crowd isn't going to don princess dresses, but breast cancer awareness offers the next best feminized fashion as women age, from pink t-shirts to pink purses to pink pajamas and underwear. Writer Barbara Ehrenreich goes so far as to call what's grown up around breast cancer a "cult—or, given that it numbers more than two million women, their families, and friends—perhaps we should say a full-fledged religion."[45] She compares pink products to talismans, races to pilgrimages, and personal narratives to religious testimonials of crisis, suffering, and salvation. Indeed, as much good as these campaigns do, a waft of hypocrisy is in the rose-colored air. Despite this hoopla to celebrate survivors and commemorate victims, Nordstrom is one of the few national retailers that carries bras for women who've had mastectomy or lumpectomy as part of breast cancer treatment.[46]

KitchenAid offers a Cook for the Cure stand mixer for the kitchen. Dick's Sporting Goods boasts pink football receiver gloves and cleats, and the National Football League offers a range of breast cancer awareness apparel and trinkets. By 2014, *Ms. Magazine,* along with the Breast Cancer Action organization and its Think Before You Pink campaign, called October "Breast Cancer Industry Month."[47] According to that article, "Only 8 percent of the money spent on pink NFL products actually goes to cancer research, making it clear that 'A Crucial Catch' is more an attempt to pander to the public and improve the NFL's image among women viewers than it is a focus on finding a cure."[48] While 8 percent is not nothing, the Breast Cancer Action network and others also point to some companies' hypocritical ways, plopping pink on products that contain ingredients known to cause cancer or that are made through processes that contaminate the environment with carcinogens. Even though alcohol consumption may be a risk factor for breast cancer, some wineries offer a pink vintage or raise funds for the cause. Pink may appear less rosy in recent years, but pink continues to be an effective strategy toward awareness and fundraising in part because it's also become a way of doing regular business.

Complaints about pink-washing the real issues also emerged recently when "Save the Ta-Tas" became a slogan for breast cancer awareness. While men can develop breast cancer, ta-tas—breasts—stand in for women. This slogan reduces women to their ta-tas, a part standing in for the whole, something to be gazed upon and fondled by straight men. Sex sells better than cancer does, so breast cancer offers a distinctive opportunity in awareness campaigns and merchandising. No one's slapping "Untangle the Intestine" or "Save the Stomach" on T-shirts, even though one could argue that the digestive system is far more essential to healthful living than are breasts.

A pornography website did offer a sexy public service announcement for Testicular Cancer Awareness Month in 2015, but "Save the Balls" didn't really catch on as a cancer awareness slogan, even though the loss of testicles to cancer has a much greater effect on the male sex drive and ability than the removal of breasts does on the female sex drive and ability and even though it's a slogan that national sports organizations could pun easily. An internet search for that catchphrase offers results for stories about the public service announcement featuring porn star Charlotte Stokely encouraging a hands-on approach to testicular cancer screening. The search also points to a webpage with more than seven hundred pornography videos that have nothing to do with cancer screening at all.

"Save the Ta-Tas" is catchy. It's titillating. It's fun. Of course, breast cancer isn't much fun. And what if the treatment is mastectomy, surgery to remove a breast? What of the woman who loses her ta-tas to win her battle against cancer? Has she really squandered anything of such great value?

To look through the photographs of "The SCAR Project" is to witness and acknowledge young women in various phases of their treatment for and recovery from breast cancer. This collection of images—of faces and bodies shot by photographer David Jay—repositions the loss of the breast as a laudatory act of humanity instead of as a failure or a deficit. What has been forfeited is the tumor. Good riddance. The ultimate goal is—or should be—to save the woman's life. Despite great strides, breast cancer remains the number two cancer killer of women in the United States and also the second deadliest for women in the United Kingdom.

Identities

Synecdoche is a figure of speech in which the part is used to represent the whole. We refer to soldiers as *boots,* as in boots on the ground. This standing in of part for whole is a version of how cancer reshapes one's identity, how cancer becomes inseparable from identity. Soldiers are soldiers because they belong to the military; they joined the group. They were drawn to or recruited into the group and adapted their apparel, attitudes, and behavior to fit the expectations each had for the others. As other identities fall away or are overshadowed, the person becomes the soldier, and the soldier becomes the person. Likewise, a person diagnosed with a malignant tumor becomes the cancer patient.

As a child, Lucy Grealy was diagnosed with Ewing's sarcoma, a rare form of cancer in the bone. Part of her jaw was surgically removed, and she underwent chemotherapy and numerous reconstruction surgeries, all of which left her face disfigured. People could see that something had happened to her and couldn't help but notice the difference between her face and most faces—sometimes, she had a metal rod protruding—and that undoubtedly shaped all her interpersonal interactions. The cancer might have killed her; instead, it changed the way she looked and, therefore, who she was and was perceived to be in the world. She writes, "The singularity of meaning—I *was* my face, I *was* ugliness—though sometimes unbearable, also offered a possible point of escape. . . . Everything led to it, everything receded from it—my face as personal vanishing point."[49] The cancer never returned, but the evidence of it having existed was there for all the world to see.

Many cancers, of course, are not evident on the surface. We don't see each other's lungs or brain, though one might glimpse someone's surgical scar underneath shirt or hat. We don't really know our own pancreas well, but, if part of it is removed to rid ourselves of a tumor, we will see the scar left, and we will feel the effects of its absence, the difficulty digesting and the lack of insulin. With the physical change ensues a transformation of the self in other ways. Gubar writes after surgery for ovarian cancer, "For if the debulking means anything it signifies the subtraction of all those interests [that bulked up one's life before cancer], now subsumed by an overriding and offensive obsession with one's own physical vulnerability."[50] The disease and the treatment leave one physically altered, not exactly the same person—not the same physical object in the world—that one was before. Moreover, the cancer patient becomes differently aware of her own physicality and the fragility of her physical self. Work, friends, hobbies tend to pale when one has difficulty keeping the body healthy and alive.

In the late 1970s, Henri Tajfel and John Turner proposed social identity theory and then self-categorization theory to explain how we arrange ourselves in groups, how those groups interact with each other, and how a person's sense of self emerges from the social groups with which that person identifies.[51] Gubar identified herself as part of the professoriate, for instance, which explains some of her values and behaviors and from which she drew self-esteem. She undoubtedly valued and felt good about teaching and contributing to intellectual culture, and others valued or criticized her on those grounds as well. She chose to identify with the professoriate as much as the professoriate chose to include her. Gubar did not choose to join the group of people with cancer, but she found herself its member nonetheless. She identified herself in this social group of those with cancer, and others, whether healthy or ill themselves, identified her this way as well.

Such identification among cancer patients can bring with it comfort and camaraderie within the group, a *me-too* sense of belonging despite one's perceived vulnerability. The teal ribbons, the September campaign for awareness, the walks to break the silence and raise research money, the local chapter meetings, the slogan—With Action, There Is Hope—are aspects of this camaraderie and group belonging for those with ovarian cancer.

Yet with the sense of belonging to the group of people who have cancer comes the sense of not belonging to the group of people who do not have cancer, even though one may have been a member of that group for decades. Moreover, those who don't have cancer may distance themselves, a *not-me* social act. Susan Sontag, in *Illness as Metaphor,* writes of illness as "a more onerous citizenship. Everyone who is born holds dual citizenship, in the kingdom of the well and the kingdom of the sick."[52] Christopher Hitchens, too, talked of the role of cancer in social identity and self-categorization through the metaphor of geography. "The new land is quite welcoming in its way. . . . The country has a language of its own—a lingua franca that manages to be both dull and difficult and that contains names like ondansetron, for anti-nausea medication—as well as some unsettling gestures that require a bit of getting used to."[53] In this new social group, which Hitchens refers to as "the sick country"[54] and "Tumortown,"[55] the new identity demands learning a new language, hearing a lot of (often unsolicited) advice, and adapting his behaviors, sometimes vomiting discreetly between job obligations.

Gubar also talks of the quick transition from the person she was to the debulked woman she became as the result of cancer and its treatment: "How could she possibly have been the active professional she thought herself to have been a few days ago when she had juggled teaching and research, grocery shopping and cooking, traveling and lecturing, mentoring and the chairing of administrative committees? Those selves have been peeled off and lie discarded in a litter of ruin behind me."[56] Gubar's social identities as professor and as wife shifted; she became a different version of professor, a different version of wife. She quickly became a former committee chair and a mother with cancer. The ways she defined herself and others defined her based on the formal and informal groups—university, neighborhood, family—to which she belonged and her relationships within those social contexts became layered by the often unspoken label of cancer.

Gubar explains, in the preface to her most recent book, *Reading & Writing Cancer*, "Surgery, radiation, and chemotherapy can cause patients to feel so invaded, so bombarded, so infused that they lose a sense of their own agency, of subjectivity, even of language."[57] She began writing about her experience to enable "a reconstitution of the self—probably not the same self that existed before diagnosis, but nevertheless another authentic self and voice. Be it angry or sorrowful, defiant or resigned, courageous or fearful, this emergent voice helps us understand who we are becoming."[58] Even without active medical treatment, there exists no way to avoid becoming a cancer patient after diagnosis, only ways to understand the transformation of self and of self among others.

The question *How are you?*—for instance—never sounds the same again, and the cancer patient tends to keep track of the answer all the time, even as the initial novelty of the diagnosis wears off. Kelly Corrigan, who wrote of her own breast cancer diagnosis and successful treatment and her father's simultaneous cancer treatment in *The Middle Place,* captures the sense that cancer becomes not just a distraction in or from one's day-to-day life but a thought that's always on one's mind in life's daily-ness as well as in moments of health crisis. Like Gubar, Corrigan identifies herself as an information seeker long before her diagnosis and brings that quality to bear on understanding the transformation of self in addition to the practical matters of decisions she must make about her own care and those her father, too, must make, sometimes differently. One evening, when she goes to her computer to check yet one more "cancer thing" online, her husband comments, "Lately, it's all cancer, all the time around here." She doesn't disagree and instead admits to herself, "All he wants is for me to stop. Everyone wishes I would just stop, including me." [59] But she cannot stop. She does not want to miss some helpful tidbit of information that might change the course of her own treatment or offer her father greater odds in his. Though she doesn't state it outright, she is also wrestling with ways to understand her transformed self and the possibilities for this new self and voice in the future. Cancer—her own and her father's—has become a filter through which she lives her life, and she cannot get enough of it. While her life is many other things as well, her life is cancer, and cancer is her life. Of her marriage, she concludes, "We are alone, together." [60] No matter the interwoven, interplaying qualities and identities, the cancer diagnosis and the treatment that follows require everyone around Corrigan to adjust, too.

While caring for her mother, who's been diagnosed with metastatic colorectal cancer in her mid-fifties, Meghan O'Rourke grapples not only with the ways her mother's body has been transformed by the disease and its treatment, but also with the ways in which cancer has changed her mother's attitudes and relationships. When her mother "went tense with anger and frustration," O'Rourke "thought of her when she was happy—her voice the night before when she said, 'I love you to death'—and I wondered which was the real her. The other, I thought. But her anger was so vivid, it was easy to believe this was the unmasked truth: She was dying, and she hated us."[61] The cancer patient may have both the old authentic voice and an emergent voice that is also authentic. Emotional responses can change from day to day, minute by minute, so that the self keeps shifting as it tries to find its new footing. Cancer often requires both the patient and those around her—family, caregivers, friends, colleagues—to hold in their minds two contradictory thoughts: anger and gratitude, grief and hope, dying and living.

Contradictory thoughts nudge a person to choose which is the truth, the real truth, and nothing but the truth, as if two things cannot be the case simultaneously. Was the person with cancer really this way all along, or has the cancer transformed her into someone else? Cancer illuminates the inherent instability of our true selves and the ways our identities are shaped by the contexts and conditions in which we live as much as they are determined by what we think of as inherently or essentially us. Both versions—the person before diagnosis and after—are authentic, genuine, true.

S. Lochlann Jain also writes of this swift shift in social roles when she was diagnosed with cancer. "I didn't know the least thing about my new role. I could more or less enact curiosity-driven researcher, loving girlfriend, stern teacher, doting Mima, dependable big sister, cash-strapped daughter, fun-loving chum, polite dinner guest, competent student, active teammate . . . but sick patient? Not in my repertoire."[62] Even as the physical body itself creates the new role, the social context of hospitals and infusion suites shows the individual how to play the sick patient, offers her costume and script. One's repertoire inevitably expands to include sick patient, and, often, the other roles one inhabited for years cannot be played with the same inflection after diagnosis.

The person does not need or even want cancer, but cancer needs the individual. Hitchens writes, "To exist, a cancer needs a living organism, but it cannot ever *become* a living organism. Its whole malice—there I go again—lies in the fact that the 'best' it can do is to die with its host."[63] Though one does not become cancer, or vice versa, in a literal sense, to live with a malignant tumor is to be and be perceived as a person with cancer. The person with cancer is a survivor and a victim. Fighters, warriors, travelers through Tumortown, citizens in the kingdom of the sick, the walking dead—all members of the club. Or as Radner remarks, "Once you've had this disease, it goes on your whole life."[64]

The lifetime risk of developing cancer—the incidence rate—is one of two for men and one in three for women, but the lifetime risk of dying from cancer—the mortality rate—is about half that. Overall survival rates are significantly better than they were a couple of decades ago. That's good news.

Moreover, though cancer risk increases with age, most of us will never be diagnosed with cancer. If one is diagnosed, much depends on the cancer type and stage as well as the individual's health. Still, almost half of people diagnosed with cancer die from some other cause, not from this emperor of all maladies. In fact, according to the Centers for Disease Control and Prevention, heart disease accounts for more deaths than does cancer in the United States (though cancer edges out heart disease in the United Kingdom).[65] Millions of people are living with or beyond cancer, carrying the diagnosis, sometimes carrying the disease, with them the rest of their lives.

4 PART AND PARCEL

Screening

The word *screen* is one of those strange words—a contranym or auto-antonym—that can mean one thing and a somewhat opposite thing. When one screens, one may obscure the view of something by covering it with a barrier. One puts screens on the windows of a house in order to keep insects out, and such a screen is a filter through which one looks out at the world. On the other hand, when one screens, one may examine something carefully and systematically to look for some specific characteristic. To screen is either to conceal or to reveal, to deter or to discover.

Cancer screening is this systematic searching, an attempt to reveal malignancy before the individual exhibits symptoms of the disease. In most cases, the earlier a tumor is detected, the easier it is to treat and the more likely the patient is to survive for a long time. So if the means exist to see a tumor before a person is aware that anything is amiss, why not take a careful look? The annual Pap test for cervical cancer starting at age twenty-one; the mammogram for breast cancer starting at age forty-five; the colonoscopy for colorectal cancer at age fifty, then repeated every ten years; the CT scan for lung cancer at age fifty-five if the individual is a heavy smoker: These are the screening methods most likely to prevent cancer deaths across a large population.

The benefits of such screening regimens statistically outweigh the risks posed by the screening itself. Both mammography and computed tomography (CT) expose the body's tissue to ionizing radiation, the stronger of the two radiation types, strong enough to change the structure of molecules by not only exciting electrons but removing an electron. The nonionizing radiation of light, heat, radio waves, and microwaves is much less dangerous to the body's tissues. Of course, we're exposed to ionizing radiation every day all the time, from the cosmic radiation of the universe and the radon that seeps from the Earth. As we breathe the air, drink the water, and eat the plants and animals around us, our bodies themselves harbor radioisotopes. Some occupations, such as uranium miner, astronaut, or even airline pilot or flight attendant, put people in greater contact with natural or other background ionizing radiation. The largest source of man-made ionizing radiation to which most of us are exposed, however, is medical imaging.

The American Cancer Society estimates, "The dose of radiation used for a screening mammogram of both breasts [two views each] is about the same amount of radiation a woman would get from her natural surroundings over about seven weeks."[1] If a women begins mammography at age forty-five and, as recommended by the American Cancer Society, continues screening every year through age fifty-four and then every other year thereafter, she will have twenty mammograms—and the equivalent of an extra one hundred forty weeks of day-to-day background radiation exposure—by the time she is seventy-four. Such a woman would have the radiation exposure equivalent to a woman almost three years older who'd never had a mammogram. Though x-rays are known human carcinogens, that fact about mammogram risk doesn't seem to matter much over a large population over time. Still, in theory and without direct cause-and-effect evidence, mammography will cause, over time, one breast cancer in every thousand women.[2] In addition, newer tomosynthesis, or 3D, technology increases radiation exposure, and women with dense or extremely dense breasts—who are at greater risk of developing cancer and whose breasts are more difficult to see via mammogram—may have mammograms with more than two views each time.

The more immediate, measurable risks of harm from routine screening mammography, however, lie instead in our suspicious nature and our desire to treat whatever appears abnormal. Screening leads to careful enough looking that benign anomalies are found and biopsied, and cancers that may never spread are found and treated. Ten percent of women screened are recalled for further testing.[3] In fact, the National Cancer Institute (NCI) suggests that 54 percent of all breast cancers and 20 percent of breast cancers detected via screening represent over-diagnosis.[4] In other words, the careful and systematic looking for something reveals something worth viewing even more closely. This additional scrutiny often means an MRI, which is expensive, and a biopsy, which is invasive. Most often, the abnormal something is almost nothing, as 95 percent of those women recalled for further testing will not be diagnosed with cancer.[5]

I have been recalled on several screening occasions. Looking more closely finally revealed enough of something— not cancer, but not nothing—that I now alternate a mammogram and an MRI, one screening every six months in a plan of heightened scrutiny that leads me to believe that it's only a matter of time before the cancer for which the radiologist is looking will appear on the screen, the search coming to fruition. This inkling of inevitability created by scrutiny flies in the face of statistics. The word *scrutiny* comes from the Latin meaning *to search*, with etymological suggestion that scrutiny is search through trash in hopes of finding something of value. Despite my increased risk, I am twice as likely not to develop breast cancer as I am to eventually face that diagnosis.

Screening is most widely helpful when the risk is high. Now that I live in the almost desert of Southern California instead of in Illinois with its humid summers and storm seasons, I don't have screens on the windows of my house. Window screens do not keep the ubiquitous spiders out anyway, and the occasional mosquito or moth isn't bothersome. Screens are needed in some geographical regions more than in others and, even in places with lots of insects, are needed in warm weather more than in cold. The decision whether to screen—a house or a body—should be made with the situation and context in mind.

For these reasons, science writer Christie Aschwanden, when given an order from her gynecologist to have her first screening mammogram at age forty, chose not to go through with it. Using the NCI's risk calculator, she determined that, with her family history, she faced an average risk and "an 89 percent probability of remaining free of breast cancer from now until age 90. Those are odds I can live with."[6] Her research led her to conclude that screening mammograms for women in their fifties reduce risk of death by only a smidge, by less than 10 percent, and that's not enough benefit, in her assessment, to offset the possibility of over-diagnosis. If she had a higher risk of breast cancer, perhaps a family history of the disease, she might come to a different conclusion. Only in recent years, once cancer screening became more commonplace, have discussions actively challenged this standard of care across populations and suggested that individualized decision-making about cancer screenings is necessary.

Mammograms, of course, are used for diagnosis as well as screening, and that distinction is important. My mother kept up with annual screening mammograms, but her breast cancer was diagnosed when she felt a lump several months after her screening mammogram. Such an interval cancer—one discovered between screenings—isn't unusual.

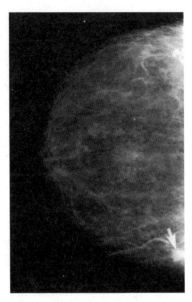

FIGURE 4.1 Mammogram image of a breast, with obvious cancer indicated by an arrow.
Source: Dr. Dwight Kaufman, National Cancer Institute.

Whenever a woman feels a lump, especially after the age of forty, her physician is likely to order mammography and ultrasound to take a careful look. That x-ray and ultrasound are diagnostic because the lump has already been located, and the mammogram is likely to involve additional views, perhaps more angles and a close-up. Whereas screening is a careful look to see if something abnormal is there, diagnosis is a careful look at something known to be there to determine whether it is abnormal. It's a difference akin to the one between wandering around a city you don't know well to happen upon a good restaurant just as you realize it's time for lunch and using a map when already hungry to find the restaurant a trusted friend has recommended.

Poison, or the other devil

Poison originally referred to *a drink*, and, even now, we ask what alcoholic beverage a companion might desire by saying, "Name your poison." In *Othello*, Shakespeare referred several times to drink, particularly wine, as the devil. One of the primary ways cancer is treated is via a toxic chemical cocktail, facing one devil with another, fighting fire with fire (as Shakespeare also suggested) in hopes that the whole body doesn't go up in flames. Forest firefighters, in fact, set purposeful, controlled burns to eliminate fuel that would feed an expanding fire so that a form of the threat itself is used to contain the threat and heal the landscape.

In his Nobel lecture in 1908, Paul Ehrlich, who is generally considered the father of chemotherapy, said, "It is, I think, a generally acknowledged and undisputed fact that everything which happens in the body, assimilation, disassimilation, must ultimately be attributed to the cell alone; and furthermore, that the cells of different organs are differentiated from each other in a specific way and only perform their different functions by means of this differentiation."[7] This generally acknowledged and undisputed fact hadn't always been a way to understand the human body, but the microscope came into wider use in the late seventeenth century and moved the study of disease from a focus on anatomy to a close-up view of the body's smallest functioning parts, the cells. Ehrlich had developed ways to stain tissues in order to see the body's cells and the parts of cells more distinctly. He was able to see differences among like cells as no one had before, and began categorizing types of blood cells as well as detecting types of typhoid in urine samples. He also explained the way that cells might survive a toxin and produce antibodies, which was the pioneering work in the field of immunology that, in large part, led to his Nobel prize.

At the end of his speech, Ehrlich touted the possibility of a magic bullet for each disease: "a *complete* cure with *one* injection, a result which corresponds to what I call *therapia sterilisans magna*."[8] This phrase describes using a large enough dose of a toxic remedy to destroy an infection or disease without seriously harming the patient. Though it often falls short of a magic bullet in application, this approach underlies chemotherapy, the treatment with toxic chemicals to combat cancer and some benign growths such as desmoid tumors.

Because each chemotherapy drug works in a distinct way during a phase of cell growth, the combination of drugs and the timing of chemo treatment are crucial to effectiveness. Oxaliplatin is an alkylating agent that works by damaging a cell's DNA so that it doesn't reproduce; 5-fluorouracil is an antimetabolite that substitutes for parts of normal DNA and RNA during the phase when cells are making copies of DNA and RNA in preparation for cell division; and irinotecan interferes with enzymes, specialized proteins that the cell uses to separate strands of DNA. These drugs, however, don't distinguish between malignant and benign cells; they poison across the board because, after all, the tumor is part and parcel of the body. Oxaliplatin results in neuropathy in the hands and feet as well as mouth sores. While anti-emetic—anti-nausea—medication is also administered to patients, 5-FU (which suggests the other use of the colloquial *FU* in treating cancer) can cause nausea, vomiting, and diarrhea and gives the mouth a metallic taste during infusion. Blood cell counts may dip as well. Toxicity of these drugs can be life threatening.

Erlich's goal of complete cure with one injection, therefore, is tricky to achieve in chemotherapy treatment for cancer because the doses necessary to destroy cancer harm the patient as well. This issue is of particular concern to former head of NCI and later the Yale Cancer Center, Vincent DeVita, who found that, in the early days of chemotherapy use, "Though I'd spelled it [meticulous dosing and scheduling of the treatment] out carefully, many doctors—in major cancer centers, in academic medical centers, and in private practice—uniformly altered the dosing or schedule of the drugs."[9] In an attempt to minimize side effects through lower doses and longer gaps between infusions, physicians had made both the chemotherapy treatment less effective and the individual's cancer more resistant to the treatment.

Cancer suggests a matter of time, in terms of the chance of developing it in the first place, the prognosis for life span once diagnosed, and the possibility of the next breakthrough in prevention or treatment. Time is an abstraction for which a cancer diagnosis suggests tangible limits, as if diagnosis starts a clock ticking toward mean survival. Cancer treatment, too, revolves around timing, as it aims to hit the cells hard enough and often enough that they cannot recover. The patient's life often becomes delineated by and organized around the routine of chemotherapy or radiation treatment and, if all goes well, the regularly scheduled check-ups for recurrence.

Because these drugs are incredibly toxic, with side effects like nausea and hair loss and the possibility that they will leave the body as decimated and at risk of infection or even death as the disease itself, physicians had wanted to schedule the administering of chemotherapy with plenty of time for the patient to recover before the next dose. DeVita and others, because of their understanding of cell phases and the effects of combinations of drugs, pushed for an unrelenting approach. While the patient recovered between treatments, so did the cancer cells. Moreover, surviving cancer cells adapted, making the drugs less effective over time. In order to eliminate all cancer, neither cancer nor patient could be given time to fully recover before the next toxic bombardment. The word *toxic*, in fact, comes from the Greek for *the poison put on the tip of an arrow*, and chemo becomes such a weapon, a drip-drip from the tip of a needle into the vein toward the enemy that is tumor.

In the late 1960s, a four-year study of a chemo combination indicated the rate of complete remission—no evidence of the disease, slightly different than cure—in Hodgkin's lymphoma was a whopping 80 percent, and that the rate of relapse was declining as time went on for the patients in the study.[10] Hodgkin's disease, which isn't a tumor in the sense of a well-defined solid growth, is now considered among the most curable of cancers, and part of the reason is that researchers like DeVita recognized "that if you looked under the microscope at the lymph nodes taken from Hodgkin's patients, the malignant cells were surrounded by infection-fighting white blood cells, lymphocytes, and other cells associated with inflammation. The cancer cells were actually in the minority. . . . It occurred to [DeVita] that even when a patient has advanced disease, the actual number of cancer cells was probably relatively small."[11] Because the total number of cancer cells seemed more manageable than in other cancers, researchers saw Hodgkin's disease as a good candidate for successful treatment via chemotherapy in ways other cancers could never be. In theory, they surmised, fewer cells meant a given amount of chemo would kill a greater percentage of those cells and the total could be reduced and reduced again before the body became overwhelmed by the toxicity of the drugs. Not everyone survives Hodgkin's disease, and those early successful efforts with chemotherapy and radiation led to some serious long-term side effects, including heart problems and secondary cancers. A new four-drug (and a newer seven-drug) combination chemotherapy administered in several carefully timed cycles—usually with a treatment spaced every two weeks in a twenty-eight day cycle—has given patients a significant survival advantage in what's close to Ehrlich's vision of *therapia sterilisans magna.*[12]

Telling time, wasting time, killing time

When oncologists offer treatment based on what researchers call *survival advantage*, the advantage may lead to a cure, as is possible in Hodgkin's lymphoma, or the advantage may be measured in weeks. Time becomes framed by statistics as well as by individual experiences of cancer.

DeVita states bluntly that more time is his primary, almost singular, goal: "I want to keep patients going until the next new treatment comes along so that they can take advantage of it."[13] He is concerned that physicians are not doing enough, not trying everything and anything in the face of even terrible odds, in order to buy more time for each patient. He thereby positions diminishment in quality of life as merely a temporary state during which patients suffer for the greater good, which he defines as quantity of life and the possibility that the patient will live long enough to benefit from the next breakthrough.

In *Being Mortal,* surgeon Atul Gawande discusses the problem of such valuing of quantity—time—over quality of life in the terminally ill. He discusses in detail the lengths physicians tend to go to keep a patient going. As an example of what he perceives as a widespread focus by physicians on keeping the patient alive at all costs—the focus DeVita thinks is largely lacking, not widespread—Gawande recounts the story of a young woman with metastatic lung cancer. "Step by step," he writes, "Sara ended up on a fourth round of chemotherapy, one with a miniscule likelihood of altering the course of her disease and a great likelihood of causing debilitating side effects."[14] What Gawande finds problematic is not the treatment itself but, rather, the narrow focus on the next treatment option and then the next—the step-by-step nature of a discussion focused entirely on medical treatment. This primary goal of keeping the patient alive squeezed out almost all consideration of the likely progression of the disease, the progression through less and less effective treatments, Sara's declining quality of life, and the ways in which the end of her life might and did play out.

Gawande criticizes the sort of optimism and determination DeVita espouses when he points to a study in which physicians tended to overestimate, sometimes drastically, their patients' survival time, particularly when they knew the patients well, and another study in which "more than 40 percent of oncologists admit to offering treatments that they believe unlikely to work."[15] This attitude suggests that physicians believe they are at Lake Wobegone General Hospital, in the imaginary town Garrison Keillor created on the radio, where all the kids are above average and all the cancer patients beat the statistical mean even as the disease advances and their health deteriorates. Whereas DeVita worries that physicians are too pessimistic and withhold treatment options, Gawande worries that physicians overcompensate for their pessimism, offer excessive and possibly harmful options, and hinge their hope on the long tail of those who, statistically, live well beyond the mean survival time.

Reading DeVita's account of how he oversaw the treatment of his friend's prostate cancer, I cannot help but notice how often the sentences use *I* as the subject, recounting the physician's control of the decision-making and treatment plan, as if playing a cancer game himself as much as keeping his friend in the game of life. The battle to keep that patient alive is construed as the physician's battle, a professional and personal challenge to which DeVita continually rises. When talking about those who believe aggressively treating advanced—metastatic—cancer isn't worth it, he argues, "When a doctor says that, what he usually means is that it's not worth it for him."[16] His stance is quite different than Gawande's, and DeVita ignores recent studies that indicate palliative care for the terminally ill leads to less treatment, less suffering, and increased survival.[17] Though he goes on to assert that physicians are largely unable to put themselves in their patients' shoes, DeVita blurs his own goals with those of his patients, concluding about additional chemotherapy for extremely frail but functional patients,

"We don't lose anything by trying this."[18] While the response to chemotherapy may be worth the side effects and give the patient additional time—while an individual may beat the mean—patients like my mother may still have something left to lose.

After my mother healed from the surgery during which her tumor was not able to be removed, her oncologist started treatment with FOLFIRINOX, a combination of several drugs—oxaliplatin, fluorouracil, irinotecan, and leucovorin—that are designed to work in conjunction to shrink the tumor, which, in turn, alleviates cancer-related symptoms, and to delay metastasis. This combination is standard care for metastasized pancreatic cancer in otherwise relatively healthy patients and is touted as successful because it extends the patient's life four months longer than the other, less toxic chemotherapy option. In other words, patients with matastisized pancreatic cancer who undergo FOLFIRINOX treatment every two weeks for at least three months tend to live 11.1 months after diagnosis.[19] My mother, whose cancer hadn't yet metastasized when she began chemo, lived less than ten months after diagnosis.

Over the course of this treatment, my mother lived with numb hands, mouth blisters, vomiting, and incontinence. The last two treatments caused more immediate and severe reactions, and she became so frail that she fell twice, fracturing her pelvis just when she otherwise would have had a couple of months of relative respite after completing the six-infusion round of chemo. While she did not develop acute pain that can accompany growing tumors and while she would have grown weaker whether or not she underwent treatment, chemotherapy is a mixed bag for the terminally ill patient.

Gateway to the heart: The medical port

When my mother was diagnosed at Stage III, when her tumor had already grown into the wall of an artery, making surgical removal impossible, she decided to undergo chemotherapy not because it would extend her life—though it undoubtedly did, by weeks or even months—but because it might lessen the pain she was likely to experience as the growing tumor began to press on her organs, blood vessels, and nerves. Despite the difficult side effects of chemo, my mother's treatment was palliative, designed to make her as comfortable as possible for as long as possible.

At first, she received FOLFIRINOX via a peripherally inserted central catheter, or PICC line, a tube that's inserted in a vein in the arm and threaded up toward the heart. It was a cumbersome contraption bandaged to my mother's inner arm, interfering with her sleeves and her movement. Because the tubes extended outside her body, the PICC could easily be damaged or broken, and would often clog up unexpectedly. It also increased her risk of developing an infection; at one point, she had three infections at the same time.

When it became clear than the PICC wasn't working—besides the infections, she also suffered from blown veins in her arms—doctors placed my mother under anesthesia and implanted a medical port the size of a quarter under the skin near her collarbone.

According to the Centers for Disease Control, my mother was one of approximately 650,000 people who undergo chemotherapy treatment annually in the United States.[20] The medical port has become an integral part of treatment for many of them, especially for those who continue treatment with the idea that some cancers can be considered chronic conditions to be managed indefinitely like diabetes.

Because many chemotherapy drugs are so toxic that they easily damage smaller blood vessels and surrounding tissue, they can't be repeatedly administered via the more commonplace IV infusion into veins in the hand or arm. Ideally, chemotherapy drugs would directly enter the vena cava, a large vein leading into the heart's upper right atrium that's less easily damaged. With no valve between the vena cava and the heart's chamber, it's also as close as something can be placed to the heart. When the drugs enter there, they are drawn quickly into the heart and propelled efficiently throughout the body—less damage, faster circulation.

Earlier devices like the PICC and the Hickman, which dangles out of the body through a hole in the chest, deliver their drugs this way, and they perform relatively well for the job of administering chemotherapy. But because some parts remain outside the skin, these gadgets—besides being invitations for infection—can make everyday actions more difficult or uncomfortable. In some patients, for example, a Hickman lies in the same spot where a seatbelt would hit. Both PICC and Hickman lines also require daily flushing to keep the tubes clear—a constant reminder of illness, as well as an annoyance. What cancer care needed was some kind of transfer device for which all the parts could be placed entirely inside the body—and the medical port, which achieves these two goals, caught on quickly after its introduction in the 1980s.

Advanced Oncology Certified Nurse Rhonda Pickett remembers the pre-port days of cancer care: "Trying to find venous access on cancer patients who have had their veins violated by the best of stickers is not fun. And being on the receiving end is not fun either."[21] No matter how experienced the nurse, compromised small veins meant a dreaded, often painful, experience for everyone involved. She also pointed out that some chemotherapy drugs cause burning, scarring, or discoloration over time, permanent markers of the illness and its treatment, even if the patient fully recovers from the cancer. Pickett calls the port "a godsend for both the patient and the nurse."[22] My mother's nurses, too, heralded the device as a relief for themselves as well as for their patients. These days, everyone I know who undergoes chemo gets a port.

The word *port* evokes the image of ships sailing in with goods. It's a place where cargo is transferred from sea to land or, in reverse, sent off from one place to another. Similarly, a medical port is such a way into the body, a point of access where powerful drugs can be transferred from the world outside the body into the liquid that circulates through it. Because blood can be drawn via the port, it is also a point through which things can leave.

The flat side of the port that lies just beneath the skin near the collarbone is a self-sealing sheath of silicone. This sheath, or septum, can withstand hundreds of needle jabs, perhaps as many as 2,000 (depending on needle size, perhaps even more), without leaking or breaking down.[23] Beneath the septum is a small reservoir, and out of the back of this reservoir runs the catheter into that large vein above the heart. Some reservoirs are made of titanium, while others are stainless steel, plastic, or some combination of materials. Ports and the attached catheters can also vary in shape and size. Because the port serves one function, however, the basic design remains the same, no matter the type: sheath, portal, catheter. After implantation, the port becomes part of the body. It sits under the skin, nearly attached to the heart, intimately part of the cancer patient.

Medical objects inside the body have become more and more common. We are organic life forms, but many of us have mechanical parts. My sister has a metal plate and screws in her back. My father-in-law had his knee replaced. An aunt had a pacemaker. Some people have arterial stents to improve blood flow; others have cochlear implants to improve hearing. When such an object is inserted inside a person, it becomes a part of that person—the body puts it to use and depends on it to function optimally.

The medical port is subtly different—it's both of the body and not of the body. The port is an object of convenience for the patient and the cancer-care providers, but the body itself doesn't find the device particularly useful, nor does it become dependent on the port for any particular function. When it's no longer needed, it's removed through a simple surgical procedure. In this way, the port remains its own separate entity, even as it sits entirely inside the person's physical form.

My friend Patricia Grace King, a fiction writer, had a port during her chemotherapy treatment before surgery for breast cancer. She wrote of her experience on her blog: "I have been so hyper-fixated on my left breast and the lump in it, but now I'm aware too of my new *port*, just over my right boob and it feels like a good counterbalance. The port is there now on the right boob to fight and *kill* the cancer in the left boob. Every time I feel it—the port—I think of that, and it's good."[24] The port made Patricia feel strong, in other words, because it symbolized the action she was taking to destroy the tumor inside her. It was part of her body, at least temporarily—and part of her mindset, too, a strangely welcome addition to herself while she needed it.

Most of the time, my mother thought nothing of her port. For a cancer patient, especially for someone with a poor prognosis, the port is often low on the list of concerns. When it was time to be stuck with a needle, though, she was both aware of the port and grateful for the way it guaranteed that she would need only a single prick—a blessing for cancer patients and medical staff alike, as drawing blood from the small, compromised veins of a chemotherapy patient can be a difficult and painful process. As my mother lost weight, the port became a more prominent lump, one of many reminders of her illness—a symbol of her status as a cancer patient, separating her in a small but significant way from the person she had been a few months earlier. Occasionally, she would run her fingers absentmindedly over the port, lightly brushing the bump of skin, as if to remind herself it was there.

5 INSIDE/OUTSIDE

Cancer in the air? Cancer in the family?

In December 1952, after a series of mechanical mishaps and human miscommunication and mistakes at the NRX nuclear reactor at the Chalk River Laboratories in Deep River, Ontario, a million gallons of radioactive water—a carcinogenic soup—stood in the basement of the building where the reactor was housed. A twenty-eight-year-old US Navy officer named Jimmy Carter had top-secret clearance and accompanied a maintenance crew on a train to Canada to help with the cleanup that would take months.

It's generally accepted now, though it was not as clear then, that any increase in exposure to radioactivity increases risk of cancer. Carter's young age and his high exposure to ionizing radiation put him at increased risk, particularly for leukemia. However, exposure to radioactivity—the type of radiation in which atomic nuclei decay—is a probabilistic risk factor rather than a deterministic risk factor. In other words, there exists no dose of radioactivity beyond which it is certain to cause cancer in every individual. Instead, radiation-induced cancer is a random process that plays out over years and over populations, so that it is almost impossible to determine which individual cancers—or which cancer deaths—are a result of radiation exposure. Risk is the uncertainty of maybe/maybe-not.

The link between exposure to radioactive substances and leukemia was first documented among survivors of the atomic bombings of Japan and also emerged in the wake of the Chernobyl nuclear power plant accident that occurred in 1986. In the aftermath of the accident, twenty-eight cleanup workers died of acute radiation syndrome, and dozens more suffered from radiation toxicity that causes symptoms such as nausea and blood cell count drops within a day or so of exposure. Twenty years after what is still considered the worst nuclear accident, the World Health Organization noted, "Recent investigations suggest a doubling of the incidence of leukaemia among the most highly exposed Chernobyl liquidators [350,000 clean-up workers]."[1] Yet there exists no way to know which cancer iterations are caused by the cleanup efforts and which would have occurred anyway.

In his book *Why Not the Best?* Carter describes the preparation for the dangerous work he did at Chalk River: "We all went out on the tennis court, and they had an exact duplicate of the reactor on the tennis court. We would run out there with our wrenches and we'd check off so many bolts and nuts."[2] They practiced on a model so that they could do the work as quickly as possible once inside the building, and, when their work began in earnest, the model was used to track progress, with each bolt and nut removed on the model as soon as it was removed on the reactor itself. When the men went into the building, they worked as fast as they could for only very short stints.

As Carter relays, "We had absorbed a year's maximum allowance of radioactivity in one minute twenty-nine seconds."[3] Six months later, Carter's urine was still radioactive.

On April 1, 1979, then-president Jimmy Carter toured the Three Mile Island nuclear power plant, just days after the partial meltdown of a nuclear reactor there. Serendipitously, the accident occurred within two weeks of the release of the feature film *The China Syndrome*, in which a nuclear power plant suffers an accident. Though not as bad as Chernobyl, the Three Mile Island accident was the worst nuclear accident in the United States. The cleanup took twenty-four years. No link between the accident and increases in cancer incidence among nearby residents has been established.

Jimmy Carter's father and all three of the former president's siblings died of pancreatic cancer. James Earl Carter Sr. died in 1953 at the age of fifty-eight. Billy Carter died in 1981 at the age of fifty-one. Ruth Carter died in 1983 at the age of fifty-four. Gloria Carter Spann died in 1990 at the age of sixty-three. Even Carter's mother developed breast cancer that metastasized to her pancreas. The family history of pancreatic cancer was so strong that, for a while, Jimmy Carter underwent twice-yearly CT scans to screen for the disease and then switched to MRIs because of the increased risk of cancer due to the radiation exposure of repeated CT scans.[4] Carter's physicians seemed pretty sure that he was teetering between not-cancer and cancer and required regular observation to confirm his body's state.

I'm reminded of the imagined cat Erwin Schrödinger put in a sealed box with a small amount of radioactive material and a vial of poison. When the first atom decays in the radioactive substance, the poison is released, and the cat, of course, dies. After an hour, then, surely the cat is dead. However, over the course of an hour, it's possible either that an atom decayed or that no atom decayed. Until we look inside the box, the result is indeterminate, riddled with uncertainty so that the cat is thought, by Schrödinger, to be both dead and alive, inhabiting both equally probable states. His point was, in part, that microscopic indeterminacy translates into macroscopic indeterminacy and that direct observation provides certainty.

(Interestingly, and as an aside, Schrödinger provides an excuse for my very writing of this book and for my grappling to understand an object that may be too unwieldy to grasp fully. In *What Is Life?* he writes, "We feel clearly that we are only now beginning to acquire reliable material for welding together the sum total of all that is known into a whole; but, on the other hand, it has become next to impossible for a single mind fully to command more than a small specialized portion of it. I can see no other escape from this dilemma (lest our true who aim be lost for ever) than that some of us should venture to embark on a synthesis of facts and theories, albeit with second-hand and incomplete knowledge of some of them—and at the risk of making fools of ourselves."[5] As he suggests at the end of that preface, the human tendency to ponder death must be offset—through this venture of writing that synthesizes facts and ideas, even when necessarily partial—by a meditation on life.)

A CT scan, in fact, is the equivalent of a year's exposure to day-to-day radiation in our environment. Surprisingly, understanding the cancer risk from now widespread medical imaging is extraordinarily difficult, with the standard reference point 25,000 survivors of the atomic bombings in Japan, most of whom were exposed to the equivalent of one to three CT scans.[6] Using this group as a reference point makes for shaky connections to CT scans, since atomic bomb survivors were subjected to whole body radiation and CT scans are usually done on a part of the body. In addition, because of the probabilistic nature of cancer incidence, the reference group doesn't provide a clear answer on which cancers were caused by the exposure. While the general attitude is that no amount of exposure to radiation is completely safe, emergency room doctors tend to think a CT scan poses no risk.[7] Two other studies suggest, on the other hand, "29,000 future cancer cases could be attributed to the 72 million CT scans performed in the country [United States] in 2007" and the possibility of "one extra case of cancer for every 400 to 2,000 routine chest CT exams."[8]

So, while Carter's physicians initially thought his risk of developing pancreatic cancer was high enough to outweigh the risk of CT scans, repeated scans that showed no cancer led to their rethinking as the number of CT scans started adding up. It's as if they were so sure they'd discover pancreatic cancer within a few screenings that they dismissed any risk, cost, or inconvenience of the ongoingness of screening. My mother underwent CT scans only after she was diagnosed with pancreatic cancer, to track the progression of the disease. Already in her seventies and not expected to live more than a year, the risk of radiation exposure from medical imaging didn't matter because radiation-induced cancer usually takes up to a decade and as long as forty years to develop. If, as his oncologist suspected, my father's exposure to ionizing radiation during his military service caused his liver cancer, it took more than twenty years to manifest itself.

The Carter family may carry a genetic mutation that predisposes them to pancreatic cancer, and Jimmy may have been the only sibling who didn't inherit it in the roll of the DNA dice. But even an individual with such a genetic mutation may never develop the disease, for it's a probabilistic not deterministic risk factor, one that suggests uncertainty among possibilities rather than a set outcome or certain if/then. As a farming family, the Carters were also exposed to pesticides and other chemicals that might have increased their cancer risk. In addition, Jimmy was the only one of the family who didn't smoke, and smoking is a known risk factor for pancreatic cancer as well as lung cancer.

Eventually Jimmy Carter did develop cancer but not the type that ran in his family. He was diagnosed with metastatic melanoma in the fall of 2015. The leading cause of melanoma, despite other risk factors such as inherited genes, is thought to be the nonionizing radiation of sunrays that damage the DNA of skin cells, turning on oncogenesis, or rapid cell proliferation, or turning off tumor suppressor genes. His light skin tone, advanced age, and being male play a role in the probability-turned-reality as well. This less common but deadlier of the types of skin cancer had already spread to his brain and liver by the time it was discovered. Carter was ninety years old. Carter went through life's decades when a person is most likely to develop cancer without a hint of the disease.[9] The five-year survival rate for patients with Stage IV melanoma is 15–20 percent.[10] Of course, he'd already outlived by far the statistical expectancy of someone born in 1924.

Individualization

Jimmy Carter was treated with surgery to remove a tumor on his liver, with radiation to shrink lesions on his brain, and with pembrolizumab, a new immunotherapy drug approved by the FDA in September 2014 to treat melanoma and made available to patients in the United Kingdom the following March. This drug, which now has FDA approval for a few cancers, including the unresectable, metastatic melanoma that Carter has, comes in the form of a powder that is mixed with water and administered intravenously every three weeks. While it doesn't work in all melanoma patients and, in fact, shrinks tumors in only roughly one in four recipients, it shrank the lesions in Carter's brain so that the metastasis there became undetectable. No one is sure why it works so well for some patients or for some cancers and not for others, "although new research suggests that certain mutations make cancer cells more visible to the immune system" and "the drugs are most likely to work in tumors that are caused by exposure to mutation-causing carcinogens," such as melanoma caused by sun exposure and lung cancer caused by smoking.[11]

Pembrolizumab targets two genes—PD-1 and PD-L1—that produce a sort of cloaking device, allowing a cancer cell to hide in plain sight from the body's T cells. PD stands for programmed death. Cell death, or apoptosis, is a natural, highly regulated, and advantageous process in which billions of the human body's cells die every day, as opposed to the traumatic cell death of necrosis. PD-1 is a protein on the surface of the immune cell. "PD-L1 on the surface of cancer cells forms a truce-like handshake with PD-1. This calls off the immune attack, allowing the cancer to proliferate unchallenged."[12] In some cancers—presumably in Carter's—when PD-L1 expresses itself, it turns on PD-1, a receptor inhibitor, and that confuses T cells designed to attack unhealthy cells. In other words, PD-1, when turned off, allows the body to attack itself, and, when turned on, allows the body to tolerate itself. When a cancer cell turns on the PD-1 checkpoint on the T cell, the body's immune system tolerates the cancer cell. Because the handshake signals a healthy cell, the body's disease-fighting mechanism mistakes the cancer cells for friendly cells. Pembrolizumab and a few other drugs are effective in some advanced melanoma because melanoma, at least in some cases, uses this particular cloaking transaction and the drug is able to prevent the friendly handshake and allow for immune system attack. Other drugs are being developed to block PD-L1 on the cancer cell, and the possibility of combinations of treatments holds additional promise.

Because it is immunogenic—because it manipulates the immune system—melanoma invites targeted approach to drug treatment. Moreover, disrupting the tumor's ability to cloak itself lasts longer than traditional therapies because the immune system continues to recognize the unhealthy cells even as they change and adapt. As long as the cloaking or handshake is prevented, the body won't tolerate the cells that don't appear healthy, even if they don't appear exactly as they did a month or year ago. The drug resistance that can be problematic with chemotherapy treatment, therefore, doesn't seem to be an issue for immunogenic treatment.

In an even stranger approach to activating the immune system, viruses like measles and polio are being introduced into cancer cells so that the immune system destroys the cancer because it thinks it's another disease. In a sort of fighting fire with fire, the body is tricked into fighting the cancer it doesn't discern as an enemy by disguising it as a disease the body will recognize as the devil and fight off.

Manipulating the immune system is one of several traits now understood to be definitive of cancer cells, distinctive ways that cancer cells thrive that weren't well understood a couple of decades ago. For decades, researchers were on the outside looking in but now have begun to glean the cancer cell from the inside out.

What's now called targeted therapy focuses on one or more of these distinctive traits. Long-time oncology nurse Rhonda Pickett explains how new drugs target these characteristics: "Targeted therapy drugs work a variety of ways such as (1) blocking or turning off chemical signals for growth and division, (2) changing proteins in the cell environment so they die, (3) preventing new blood vessel growth, (4) prompting the immune system, or (5) carrying toxins to the cancer cell to destroy it."[13] The first of these characteristics actually points to two traits, a double whammy for successful proliferation: rapid, wild growth and elimination of the slowing system for cell growth. Most importantly, because the original tumor is not nearly as great a threat to a person's longevity as is metastasized cancer, "The budding cancer cell reactivates this ability to travel, which is another characteristic critical to the developing embryo."[14] These traits of cancer are also traits of an embryo that proliferates to form as a human being. Some targeted therapies focus on one trait, whereas others create multiple changes in the harmful cells. Healthy cells, in most instances, are spared.

In what might have been wild speculation ten years ago and is still mathematical conjecture on the way to application, researchers are conducting theoretical and computational exploration of recent experimental evidence on the structure of chromosomal variability in cancer cells. It's possible that cancer stem cells—undifferentiated cells that can produce various differentiated cells—may possess the ability to adapt the rate of a type of mutation in which chromosomes don't separate properly when the cell divides. This model suggests that cancer cells might be considered so-called quasispecies, with descendants carrying various mutations, as opposed to a species in which offspring are predominantly accurate genetic copies. A quasispecies is unstable, with no single genotype to target and, instead, different mutations here and there. If this model proves true, however, such ability to adapt and shift chromosome segregation errors is unlikely to be the product of the evolutionary history of a single, specific tumor. Instead, this cancer cell trait is more likely a trait of stem cells generally that is observed in cancer stem cells specifically. If that's the case, this quality that is present in stem cells is likely reactivated, possibly by environmental and other factors, in cancer cells. Understanding the reactivation that distinguishes cancer cells could be a new way to treating cancer because, if a cancer cell trait can be reactivated, it, presumably, can be deactivated.[15]

In other words, the traits that distinguish cancer cells from healthy cells—cloaking from the immune system, rapid and unstable cell division, and so on—have long made cancer difficult to treat, especially in relation to the tricky balance between killing cancer cells and preserving healthy cells so that the patient isn't unduly harmed. In recent years, since the turn of this century, researchers have been able to look more closely at cancer cells to figure out how to undermine their distinctive traits, to turn off the characteristics that make a cell behave and thrive as cancer. These traits have become targets, strengths recast as vulnerabilities.

While understanding molecular and cellular distinctions is a breakthrough for development of new treatments, cancer cells, however, vary in the types of changes they exhibit. The changes in a lung cancer cell and a colon cancer cell are different, and, even within a type of cancer, one person's melanoma cells may have different genetic mutations than another person's. Cancer, then, is not only a collection of types of disease but also varied within type, making the single magic bullet an impossibility.

The word *target* suggests that this treatment approach is indeed a battle, for the word goes back to the idea of the soldier's shield and, later, as *an object at which to shoot*. A targeted cancer treatment, then, aims at a particular characteristic of each individual cancer cell that not only distinguishes it from a healthy cell but also accounts for the threat it poses. Targeted therapies don't just hit cancer cells, they hit cancer cells where it hurts. A targeted treatment is the poison on the tip of a precisely aimed arrow, not the blunt bludgeoning of the body that is chemotherapy. Echoing Shakespeare's Hamlet, the cancer patient suffers the slings and arrows of his or her outrageous fortune, but these poisoned arrows are the new arms to be taken up against the sea of cancer's troubles.

(Un)Clear margin

Just as I think I know what a tumor is—the object that is you, the object that is not you—I realize that the tumor is not as distinct as I think. When a surgeon excises a tumor, the goal is a clear—clean, free, negative—margin. In other words, the surgeon is considered to have gotten it all if there are no cancer cells on the edge of what's been removed. The tissue mass that's excised is inked so that any cancer cell on its exterior can be seen by a pathologist. With the all clear of a good margin, taking more tissue is thought not to improve patient outcomes.

Yet surrounding some cancers, namely those arising from epithelial tissue—the surfaces and linings inside the body as in the breast, prostate, bladder, lung, or mouth—there exists a field effect in which cells beyond the edge of the tumor, while not malignant, exhibit molecular changes. Epithelial cells, because they reproduce frequently, seem especially susceptible to this field effect in which cells that appear structurally healthy are genetically, epigenetically, or biochemically altered. Field cancerization was first posited by researchers in 1953 to explain the popping up of separate tumors at roughly the same time[16]—multicentric origin, or multiple primary tumors—as well as the recurrence of a new tumor in the area or organ from which the primary tumor was completely excised. The concept suggests the possibility that histologically sound yet altered cells expand over a field, creating the opportunity for cancer. In other words, the cancer—the cancer potential—spreads through epithelial tissue even before it is cancer.

The question of where we end and the tumor begins—or where the body is healthy and where disease begins—is even more complicated and slippery than I'd earlier supposed. Field cancerization introduces time—when exactly does healthy end and disease begin?—and other linkages to this question. Field cancerization reminds me of the children's story "This Is the House that Jack Built:"

This is the tumor the body built;
this is the tissue that surrounds the tumor the body built;
these are the cells in the tissue that surrounds the tumor the body built;
these are the changes in the cells in the tissue that surrounds the tumor the body built;
these are the genes that caused changes in the molecules in the tissue that surrounds the tumor the body built
this is the sunlight or cigarette or . . .

And so on as this thought experiment attempts to trace a tumor's origins and the increasingly indirect etiological links.

Of course, my thought experiment is an oversimplification of cause and effect, of step-by-step progression. There exists no single reason a person develops cancer; there exist many if/then possibilities. Moreover, the NCI admits, "There has been a long-standing fascination in the differences between benign and malignant tumors, but little modern work to characterize the functional differences between these two tumor types, with very different levels of risk to patients, has been reported."[17] A tumor is a tumor, after all. While differences among tumors exist and while those differences can mean life or death, researchers do not yet adequately understand exactly what distinguishes malignant from benign, nor why some benign tumors are likely to transform into malignant tumors. We have learned only enough to know what we do not know. Being able to state what we do not know becomes a way of learning anew.

Despite this admitted not knowing exactly what malignant means, the study of field cancerization is an attempt to understand the step-by-step process by which cancer develops and suggests that there exists a range in between healthy and malignant cells. As such, this area of research applies not only to defining tumor margins and disease progression but also to risk assessment and early detection, perhaps detection of malignancy before it happens. Though one supposedly can't be a little bit pregnant, might one be a little bit malignant or soon-to-be malignant? What if cancer is not an either/or, not an on/off, but, rather, a getting warmer of always approaching?

If so, what characteristics—which gene, gene expression, or biochemical anomalies—signal field cancerization? What conditions create a field effect? And what happens to cause the field to give rise to cancer cells? Or, as the National Cancer Institute's first in a list of provocative research questions asks,

"For tumors that arise from a pre-malignant field, what properties of cells in this field can be used to design strategies to inhibit the development of future tumors?"[18]

This question asks scientists like my colleague Marco Bisoffi to identify specific cell changes in pre-malignant states, changes evident in the tumor and not present in "truly normal cells" and then to use that knowledge to design ways to prevent the development of cancer.[19] When I spoke with Bisoffi about his work, however, he said that the philosophical dilemma is in defining the truly normal cell. Indeed, since field cancerization leads us to understand that the tumor's edge isn't as clear as we thought, how can we know where the field effect ends, where the edge between pre-malignant and normal lies? Because oxidative stress on the body's tissue accumulates over time, our cells change as we age and are not in as good shape as they were a couple of decades earlier. Time instead of space—the body's age instead of the body's geography—may be the dimension in which to define normal. Cells that are normal at age twenty will be different at age sixty, but does that change make them no longer truly normal? At what age are a body's cells most normal, or does normal change as we age? At what point does a changed cell become not truly normal, particularly if all cells are changing? Is the point of not truly normal also the point of no longer healthy? It's quite possible that not all not-normal is unhealthy.

In addition, it's not yet completely clear whether field cancerization allows the tumor to emerge from it or whether the tumor causes the field effect in surrounding tissue. Which is the cause of the other? It's logical to think that the greater evil grows from the lesser, that the field gives rise to the tumor—and that's the premise of the NCI's first provocative question designed to call forth answers that lead to cancer intervention and prevention. But what if the field is generated by the tumor to hedge its bets against excision, to leave behind a future iteration if it is removed? What if the tumor changes its immediate environment as much as the environment is conducive to the tumor? If that's the case, the pre-malignant field effect would be different than the post-malignant field effect, but field cancerization has been defined, thus far, only by tissue surrounding cancerous tumors.

One concern that emerges from such pondering of pre-malignancy is that of overtreatment, particularly in prostate cancer and breast cancer that are the subjects of Bisoffi's research. Prostate cancer itself may be considered truly normal, a common side effect of aging. Analysis of twenty-nine autopsy studies conducted between 1948 and 2013 showed that 59 percent of men older than seventy-nine have prostate cancer.[20] In these men, the disease was incidental, both in the clinical sense that it was not apparent in whatever physical exams they'd had while alive and also in the colloquial sense that it was unimportant in their lives. If most eighty-year-old men have prostate cancer and die of something else without realizing they have cancer, might we question whether all cancer should be actively treated under any conditions?

The characteristics of normal, then, shift over time. Healthy is a state of being whole, the sum of our parts. The word *normal* comes from the Latin for *the carpenter's square*, a tool of right angle. Normal, then, is a shape or pattern as much as it is a rule or ruler by which to measure. *Disease* comes from words meaning *without comfort*. In an odd twist of etymology, an earlier French sense of the word *ease*, however, refers to having *elbow room*—a margin of empty space surrounding the body. Extending this linguistic pondering a bit further, the elbow is the body's carpenter square. Only, we can change its angle.

The art of cancer

A tumor is one among life's many constraints. As artists of all varieties—painters, musicians, writers—have long understood and as researchers have more recently pointed out:

> Daily life is full of obstacles. . . . Might the cognitive effects of obstacles reach beyond the very goal or task at hand? . . . We propose that unless people are inclined to disengage prematurely from ongoing activities, obstacles will prompt them to step back and adopt a more global, Gestalt-like processing style that allows them to look at the "big picture" and conceptually integrate seemingly unrelated pieces of information.[21]

While constraints appear to be restrictions or interferences, they often instead—at least when the individual sticks with the task—function as a means to creativity, open-mindedness, and innovation not only for the task at hand but more generally. In addition, studies indicate that, when we face obstacles, we tend to appreciate tasks we see through and become practiced in global—wide and inclusive—thinking whenever unexpected circumstances arise.

We might well consider ourselves artists creating our lives, pulling out our carpenter's square and putting some elbow grease into the effort. Our lives are works in progress. One might think of life and art as versions of the same process of creation. The obstacle or interference that is tumor is an unwelcome constraint on the process of living. Make no mistake: a life-threatening constraint such as cancer should not be romanticized into something necessary for a better life.

Yet, as we stick with the task of living, such a constraint as cancer refocuses us on fundamental tasks and deeply held goals and opens more expansive problem-solving. Think of the painter who runs out of one color and must remix the remaining paints or the painter who merely reaches the edge of the canvas. Consider the sculptor thumbing clumps of clay onto a form, re-shaping with a rasp, perhaps a lump or air pocket unforgiving, the clay and tool each a constraint on what's possible to accomplish and together creating opportunities otherwise un-envisioned. Think of the composer working on a sonata or the poet grappling with the compression of language that the sonnet's length, rhythm, and rhyme demand. No two sonnets are exactly alike, just as no two lives with cancer are alike.

Poet Jeannine Gailey had an array of symptoms that doctors finally surmised were caused by tumors. She writes of her recent carcinoid syndrome diagnosis: "So, I've been writing poems—even before this new cancer diagnosis—about luck. . . . I've been thinking a lot about the way we think about luck, both good and bad. Being in the wrong place at the wrong time, celebrating Bastille Day only to be run down by a terrorist, or having a scan that incidentally discovers metastasized cancer in your liver on an ER run for stomach flu—we can't control everything or protect ourselves from even the worst things we can imagine."[22] A tumor is one of the worst things we can imagine, one of the life experiences we often avoid imagining. Yet many of us will hear that diagnosis, hoping for the word *benign,* fearing the probability of *malignant.*

Poet Lucille Clifton writes of her breast cancer diagnosis, which would not be her last bout with cancer, in "1994":

i was leaving my fifty-eighth year
when a thumb of ice
stamped itself hard near my heart

you have your own story
you know about the fears the tears
the scar of disbelief

you know that the saddest lies
are the ones we tell ourselves
you know how dangerous it is

to be born with breasts
you know how dangerous it is
to wear dark skin[23]

Clifton knows her risk factors: female, post-menopausal, African-American. She knows our fear of cancer, our disbelief, our *why me?* She knows the thumb of ice near the heart, an echo of which even I have felt after my own lumpectomy for what was not cancer but might have become. Clifton died in 2010, at the age of eighty-three, outliving her initial tumor by more than twenty years.

Poet Audre Lorde wrote in *The Cancer Journals*: "What is there possibly left for us to be afraid of, after we have dealt face to face with death and not embraced it? Once I accept the existence of dying as a life process, who can ever have power over me again?"[24] While I have not been diagnosed with cancer myself, pondering the concept of tumor is my attempt to understand, as Lorde claims, that dying is a life process and to conclude as well that living is a death process. As Lorde says, "I do not want my anger and pain and fear about cancer to fossilize into yet another silence, nor to rob me of whatever strength can lie at the core of this experience, openly acknowledged and examined."[25]

My own is a very different attempt at openly acknowledging and examining the experience of tumor, at resisting silence in the face of anger, pain, fear, and sadness. Importantly, as Susan Gubar notes in *Reading & Writing Cancer*, "At the risk of stating the obvious, writing about cancer is not quite the same as having cancer. Writing puts us at a remove from the phenomena being recorded. . . . While writing, I dwell not on the here and now but on a representation of the here and now—or some there and then—that resurrects itself with a new meaning or symmetry and a different vantage."[26] In writing these words about cancer, I remove myself from cancer in order to understand it more fully.

My father started chemotherapy on my birthday and died, almost five years later, on the anniversary of the first Apollo moon landing. My mother shares her death date with the astronomer Henrietta Leavitt and the poet Robert Browning; it is the feast of Our Lady of Guadalupe. While at a remove, I continue to dwell on these events—what they might have meant to my parents, what they mean to me even years later, what they imply for others—and to find new meaning as a cell widens to a body to a life to a community to the universe. As in the short film *Powers of Ten*,[27] vantage changes scale, and the same thing is seen differently, from its tiniest components to its largest contexts.

When faced with several cancer deaths within a few years—the deaths of my mother, two college friends, my sister's best friend from high school, a friend of the family, a poet who'd become a friend, even the astronaut

Sally Ride, who died a few months before my mother of the same disease—I began writing poems to grapple with what I understood and didn't, with the difference and interconnectedness between the specific and the universal. Here, I return to the cancer in my family, to a pair of poems for my parents called "Gravity."

Gravity (1)
for my father, 1933–1986

A time comes when gravity is going to win.
The time has always been coming,
an inevitable result of mass and age
and how much is left to burn.
When the inner core has burned
one thing into another, all of the one thing
exhausted, the shell suffices for a while,
blazing. The star expands and cools.
The core reignites, shrinks;
the star fades, brightens.
A moment arrives when the shell is used up,
when a star can no longer hold up
the weight of itself.
When gravity overcomes pressure,
the star collapses, dims, no energy left.
What's left is heavy, like tons in a teaspoon,
that, if dropped on Earth from a few feet,
would travel thousands of miles an hour.

Gravity (2)
for my mother, 1940–2012

A time comes when gravity is going to win,
when the determination is made,
when my mother is determined to be gravely ill,
looking for one thing, finding a shadow nearby.
The time is coming. Time will tell. It always does.
The cancer fills her up; her insides transform.
Her belly expands; her extremities lose feeling.
My mother's days dim, then intensify,
the day-to-day of weakening, exhaustion.
She falls with the weight of herself
and her unsteady state, a state of un-being.
A moment arrives when my mother can no longer hold up.
When gravity overcomes pressure,
the lungs can't draw another breath.
The memory I have of my mother
glows like a white dwarf. She sometimes eludes
my mind's eye, but even a worried stone
dropped from my extended hand to my heart
is so heavy, it travels thousands of miles an hour.

Our human incandescence has a life span, and our demise
emerges from life itself. Tumors are the stuff of life, perhaps
not inevitable for the individual but unavoidable for the
whole of us as living creatures.

ACKNOWLEDGMENTS

Thanks to Ian Bogost and Christopher Schaberg, the editors of the Object Lessons series, for welcoming my ideas and words. Thanks also to Haaris Naqvi at Bloomsbury Publishing and to the whole team there for making this series happen. Also, thanks to those in the science section of the *Atlantic* for publishing my piece on mediports (adapted in "Part and Parcel") that started the process toward this book.

Special thanks to Alison Kinney and Antonia Malchik, two fellow writers whom I've not yet met but who cheered me on as I proposed and drafted *Tumor*. Gratitude to the many other writers who have taken on and who continue to take on cancer as their subject matter. Several of them, though far from all, appear in the endnotes.

I'm grateful to those whose feedback has shaped my nonfiction, especially Brigid Leahy, Mary Cantrell, Patricia Grace King, Audrey Petty, Kim Brown, and Paulette Livers. Writing is done in isolation, but writers depend upon community.

I hold in esteem colleagues, students, and key administrators at Chapman University for creating an environment in which ideas and connections thrive. Special thanks to Joanna Levin, Jim Blaylock, and Lisa Kendrick, who helped me juggle several roles while writing this book, and to Daniele Struppa, Lisa Sparks, and Marco Bisoffi, who talked about tumors with me.

Much of this book was drafted at Dorland Mountain Arts Colony, a place of respite for writers, artists, and musicians. Gratitude to Janice and Robert there and for their motto for all of us: *Get back to your easel!* This book was finished during a fellowship at The American Library in Paris, for which I am deeply grateful. Gratitude to Charles Trueheart, Grant Rosenberg, and the whole terrific staff there and to Charles and Clydette de Groot.

Finally, thanks to my whole family. Douglas, you continue to amaze and comfort me.

NOTES

Chapter 1

1 When referring to the etymology of words throughout this book, *Online Etymology Dictionary* was my reference point; see www.etymology.com.

2 "More Patients Will Die of Pancreatic Cancer Than Breast Cancer," Pancreatic Cancer Action Network, January 7, 2016, https://www.pancan.org/about-us/news-press-center/2016-press-releases/press-release-january-7-2016-cancer-statistics-2016-report/.

3 "Cancer Facts and Figures 2016," American Cancer Society, http://www.cancer.org/acs/groups/content/@research/documents/document/acspc-047079.pdf.

4 Note that statistics in the text are most often for the United States. Breast, lung, colon, and prostate are the most common cancers in the United States, in the United Kingdom, and worldwide. While cancer-related statistics are often roughly the same in the United Kingdom as in the United States, incidence and mortality rates vary, medical systems and treatment protocols vary from country to country, and similar statistics are not necessarily determined in the same ways. Pancreatic cancer in the United Kingdom has an overall 5 percent,

five-year survival rate, for instance, which is a few percentage points lower than in the United States, but there exists "no UK-wide statistics for pancreatic cancer survival by stage," as there does in the United States. "Survival Statistics for Pancreatic Cancer," Cancer Research UK, https://www.ons.gov.uk/peoplepopulationandcommunity/birthsdeathsandmarriages/deaths/bulletins/deathsregistrationsummarytables/2015.

5   Lola Rahib, Benjamin D. Smith, Rhonda Aizenberg, Allison B. Rosenzweig, Julie M. Fleshman, and Lynn M. Matrisian, "Predicting Cancer Incidence and Deaths to 2030," *Cancer Research* 74:11 (June 2014), http://cancerres.aacrjournals.org/content/74/11/2913.

6   "Breast Cancer Facts & Figures 2013–2014," American Cancer Society, http://www.cancer.org/acs/groups/content/@research/documents/document/acspc-042725.pdf.

7   "SEER Stats Fact Sheets: Breast Cancer," National Cancer Institute, http://seer.cancer.gov/statfacts/html/breast.html.

8   "SEER Stats Fact Sheets: Pancreas Cancer," National Cancer Institute, http://seer.cancer.gov/statfacts/html/pancreas.html.

9   "Breast Cancer Facts & Figures 2013–2014," American Cancer Society.

10   "Common Cancer Types," American Cancer Society, http://www.cancer.gov/types/common-cancers.

11   Siddhartha Mukherjee, *The Emperor of All Maladies: A Biography of Cancer* (New York: Scribner, 2010), 154.

12   "'UK Astronaut' Piers Sellers on Living with Cancer," BBC Online, January 21, 2016, http://www.bbc.com/news/uk-england-35374271.

13   Randy Pausch, "Really Achieving Your Childhood Dreams," Carnegie Mellon, YouTube, September 18, 2007, https://www.youtube.com/watch?v=ji5_MqicxSo.

14 Mukherjee, *The Emperor of All Maladies*, 154.

15 Lynn Sherr, *Sally Ride: America's First Woman in Space* (New York: Simon & Schuster, 2014), 307–308.

16 I wrote about the year I read Tolstoy's novella in college and about the connections between that book and my life in "Sweet Dreams Are Made of This," *Dogwood: A Journal of Poetry and Prose* 15 (2016): 15–32.

17 Thomas J. Papadimos and Stanislaw P. A. Stawicki, "The Death of Ivan Ilyich: A Blueprint for Intervention at the End of Life," *International Journal of Critical Illness and Injury Science* 1:2, 125–28, http://www.ncbi.nlm.nih.gov/pmc/articles/PMC3249844/.

18 Patient autonomy and cultural differences are covered in numerous articles, including the following: N. Tchen et al., "Quality of Life and Understanding Disease Status Among Patients of Different Ethnic Origins," *British Journal of Cancer* 89:4 (2003), 641–47, http://www.ncbi.nlm.nih.gov/pmc/articles/PMC2376912/; Mary S. McCabe et al., "When the Family Requests Withholding Information: Who Owns the Truth?" *Journal of Oncology Practice* 6:2 (2010), 94–96, http://www.ncbi.nlm.nih.gov/pmc/articles/PMC2835490/.

19 Ali Montezari, Azadeh Tavoli, Mohammed Ali, Mohagheghi, Rasool Rashan, and Zahra Tavoli, "Disclosure of Cancer Diagnosis and Quality of Life in Cancer Patients: Should It be the Same Everywhere?" *BMC Cancer* 9, 39, http://www.ncbi.nlm.nih.gov/pmc/articles/PMC2639611/.

20 Shekhawat Laxmi and Joad Anjum Khan, "Does the Cancer Patient Want to Know? Results from a Study in an Indian Tertiary Cancer Care Center," *South Asian Journal of Cancer* 2:2 (2013), 57–61, http://www.ncbi.nlm.nih.gov/pmc/articles/PMC3876664/.

21 Atul Gawande, *Being Mortal: Medicine and What Matters in the End* (New York: Metropolitan Books, 2014), 2–3.

22 "My Big Brother," *Scrubs,* Season 2, Episode 6, Touchstone Television, ABC.

23 Eve Ensler, *In the Body of the World* (New York: Metropolitan Books, 2013), 116–17.

24 Christopher Hitchens, *Mortality* (New York: Twelve, 2012), 7.

25 "SEER Stats Fact Sheets: Liver and Intrahepatic Bile Duct Cancer," National Cancer Institute, http://seer.cancer.gov/statfacts/html/livibd.html.

26 I wrote about my father's cancer, its possible relationship to radiation exposure, and the Cold War in "Strange Attraction: John Wayne and Me," *The Southern Review* (Spring, 2011), 313–28.

27 "The 1973 Fire, National Personnel Records Fire," National Archives, http://www.archives.gov/st-louis/military-personnel/fire-1973.html.

28 "Radiation Compensation Exposure Act," US Department of Justice, https://www.justice.gov/civil/common/reca.

29 Michael F. Sorrentino, Jiwon Kim, Andrew E. Foderaro, and Alexander G. Truesdell, "5-Fluorouracil Induced Cardiotoxicity: A Review of the Literature," *Via Medica* 19:5, 453–58, https://journals.viamedica.pl/cardiology_journal/article/viewFile/22956/18191.

30 "SEER Stats Fact Sheets: Liver and Intrahepatic Bile Duct Cancer," National Cancer Institute.

31 "Hyperplasia (ductal or lobular)," American Cancer Society, http://www.cancer.org/healthy/findcancerearly/womenshealth/non-cancerousbreastconditions/non-cancerous-breast-conditions-hyperplasia.

32 "Genetics of Breast and Gynecologic Cancers (PDQ)-Health Professional Version," National Cancer Institute, http://www.cancer.gov/types/breast/hp/breast-ovarian-genetics-pdq#link/_95.

33 George Johnson, *The Cancer Chronicles: Unlocking Medicine's Deepest Mystery* (New York: Knopf, 2013), 28.

34 "Body Measurements," National Center for Health Statistics, National Center for Disease Control and Prevention, http://www.cdc.gov/nchs/fastats/body-measurements.htm.

Chapter 2

1 William Shakespeare, *Romeo and Juliet,* 1.2.47–48, http://shakespeare.mit.edu/romeo_juliet/full.html.

2 "Lifetime Risk of Developing or Dying From Cancer," American Cancer Society, http://www.cancer.org/cancer/cancerbasics/lifetime-probability-of-developing-or-dying-from-cancer.

3 S. Lochlann Jain, *Malignant: How Cancer Becomes Us* (Berkeley: University of California Press, 2013), 4.

4 George Orwell, "How the Poor Die," The Orwell Prize website, *Now* 6 (1946), http://www.theorwellprize.co.uk/the-orwell-prize/orwell/essays-and-other-works/how-the-poor-die/.

5 Jain, *Malignant*, 2.

6 "Vietnam Surgery Removes Tumor Twice Man's Weight," CNN, January 8, 2012, http://www.cnn.com/2012/01/06/health/vietnam-tumor/.

7 Vellanki Venkata Sujatha and Sunkavalli Chinna Babu, "Giant ovarian serous cystadenoma in a postmenopausal woman: a case report," *Cases Journal 2,* July 23, 2009, http://www.ncbi.nlm.nih.gov/pmc/articles/PMC2740039/.

8 "Diagnosis and Treatment," The Desmoid Tumor Research Foundation, http://dtrf.org/diagnosis-and-treatment/.

9   "Malignant (adj.)," Online Etymology Dictionary, http://www.
     etymonline.com/index.php?term=malignant.

10   Susan Gubar, *Memoir of a Debulked Woman* (New York: W. W.
     Norton, 2012), 13.

11   Mukherjee, *The Emperor of All Maladies*, 38.

12   William Shakespeare, *As You Like It*, 2.7, https://www.poets.
     org/poetsorg/poem/you-it-act-ii-scene-vii-all-worlds-stage.

13   "How Is Breast Cancer Staged?" American Cancer Society,
     http://www.cancer.org/cancer/breastcancer/detailedguide/
     breast-cancer-staging.

14   Carla Malden, *Afterimage: A Brokenhearted Memoir of a
     Charmed Life* (Guilford, CT: Skirt!, 2011), 25.

15   Ensler, *In the Body of the World*, 87–88.

16   "Metastasis (n.)," Etymology Online Dictionary,
     http://www.etymonline.com/index.php?term=metastasis.

17   Malden, *Afterimage*, 99.

18   Ibid., 132.

Chapter 3

1   Mukherjee, *The Emperor of All Maladies*, 6.

2   Johnson, *The Cancer Chronicles*, 28.

3   E. Bianconi et al., "An Estimation of the Number of Cells
     in the Human Body," *Annals of Human Biology* 40:6
     (July 5, 2013), 463–71, http://www.ncbi.nlm.nih.gov/
     pubmed/23829164.

4   Christian Tomasetti and Bert Vogelstein, "Cancer Etiology:
     Variation in Cancer Risk Among Tissues Can Be Explained

by the Number of Stem Cell Divisions," *Science* 347 (January 2, 2015): 78–81, http://www.ncbi.nlm.nih.gov/pubmed/25554788.

5 Jennifer Couzin-Frankel, "The Simple Math Explains Why You May (or May Not) Get Cancer," *Science*, January 1, 2015, http://www.sciencemag.org/news/2015/01/simple-math-explains-why-you-may-or-may-not-get-cancer.

6 Ibid.

7 Ibid.

8 "SEER Stats Fact Sheets: Colon and Rectum Cancer," National Cancer Institute, http://seer.cancer.gov/statfacts/html/colorect.html.

9 "SEER Stats Fact Sheets: Brain and Other Nervous System Cancer," National Cancer Institute, http://seer.cancer.gov/statfacts/html/brain.html.

10 Jennifer Couzin-Frankel, "Bad Luck and Cancer: A Science Reporter's Reflections on a Controversial Story," *Science*, January 13, 2015, http://www.sciencemag.org/news/2015/01/bad-luck-and-cancer-science-reporter-s-reflections-controversial-story.

11 Mukherjee, *The Emperor of All Maladies*, 16.

12 Ibid., 6.

13 "Small Potatoes," *The X-Files,* 20th Century Fox, April 20, 1997.

14 Naohiku Kuno, "Mature Ovarian Cystic Teratoma with a Highly Differentiated Homunculus: A Case Study," *Birth Defects Research Part A: Clinical and Molecular Teratology,* October 28, 2003, https://www.ncbi.nlm.nih.gov/pubmed/14745894.

15 Michael Munn, *John Wayne: The Man Behind the Myth* (New York: Penguin, 2005), 257.

16 "Perceptions of Cancer in Society Must Change," *The Lancet* 17:3 (March, 2016), 257, http://www.thelancet.com/journals/lanonc/article/PIIS1470-2045(16)00091-7/fulltext.

17 Gilda Radner, *It's Always Something* (New York: Simon & Schuster, 2009), 75.

18 Ibid., 59.

19 "Perceptions of Cancer in Society Must Change," 257.

20 Susan Gubar, *Reading & Writing Cancer: How Words Heal* (New York: W. W. Norton, 2016), 7.

21 Ibid., 8.

22 Christine Lennon, "Ovarian Cancer: Fighting for a Cure," *Harper's Bazaar,* June 3, 2009, http://www.harpersbazaar.com/beauty/health/news/a391/barack-obama-ovarian-cancer/.

23 Radner, *It's Always Something*, 59.

24 Hitchens, *Mortality*, 6.

25 Ibid., 7.

26 "Loved Ones Recall Local Man's Cowardly Battle with Cancer," *The Onion,* February 24, 1999, http://www.theonion.com/article/loved-ones-recall-local-mans-cowardly-battle-with--772.

27 Emily Debrayda Phillips, Obituary, *The Florida Times Union,* March 31, 2015, http://www.legacy.com/obituaries/timesunion/obituary.aspx?n=emily-debrayda-phillips&pid=174524066&.

28 Ibid.

29 Emily Dickinson, "Because I Could Not Stop for Death," Academy Of American Poets, https://www.poets.org/poetsorg/poem/because-i-could-not-stop-death-479.

30 Gubar, *Memoir of a Debulked Woman*, 29.

31 Ibid.

32 Hitchens, *Mortality*, 89.

33 Ensler, *In the Body of the World*, 113.

34 "Staying Safe Around Bears," US National Park Service, https://www.nps.gov/subjects/bears/safety.htm

35 Italics mine. Jimmy Carter, "The State of the Union Address Delivered Before a Joint Session of Congress," The American Presidency Project, January 23, 1980, http://www.presidency. ucsb.edu/ws/?pid=33079.

36 "A Promise Renewed: Fiscal Year 2015 Annual Report," Susan G. Komen Foundation, 2015, https://ww5.komen. org/uploadedFiles/_Komen/Content/About_Us/Financial_ Reports/SGK-2015-Annual-Report-reader.pdf.

37 "We Wage Hope: 2014 Impact Report," Pancreatic Cancer Action Network, 2014, https://www.pancan.org/wp-content/ uploads/2014/12/PCAN-Impact-Report-2014-sm.pdf.

38 Return of Organization Exempt from Tax (Form 990), National Pancreatic Cancer Foundation, http://www.npcf.us/ wp-content/uploads/2014/04/F990-2015.pdf.

39 "Cancer Among Women," Centers for Disease Control and Prevention, https://www.cdc.gov/cancer/dcpc/data/women. htm.

40 "Cancer Disparities," National Cancer Institute, http://www. cancer.gov/about-cancer/understanding/disparities.

41 "Funding for Research Areas," National Cancer Institute, http://www.cancer.gov/about-nci/budget/fact-book/data/ research-funding.

42 Ibid.

43 "Current Grants by Cancer Type," American Cancer Society, http://www.cancer.org/research/ currentlyfundedcancerresearch/grants-by-cancer-type.

44 "CSR Insider's Guide to Peer Review," Center for Scientific Review, National Institutes of Health, http://public.csr.nih.gov/aboutcsr/NewsAndPublications/Publications/Pages/InsidersGuide.aspx.

45 Barbara Ehrenreich, "Welcome to Cancerland," *Harper's Magazine,* November 2001, 43–53.

46 Breast Prosthesis Program, Nordstrom, http://shop.nordstrom.com/c/prosthesis-program.

47 Rachel Kassnebrock, "Breast Cancer Industry Month Is Here!" *Ms. Magazine*, October 13, 2014, http://msmagazine.com/blog/2014/10/13/breast-cancer-industry-month-is-here/.

48 Ibid.

49 Lucy Grealy, *Autobiography of a Face* (New York: Harper Perennial, 1994), 7.

50 Gubar, *Memoir of a Debulked Woman*, 89.

51 In addition to how I discuss social identity and self-categorization theories here, scholars are exploring ways in which these dynamics affect patient care. For instance, oncologists may use social identity to stereotype a patient in ways detrimental to positive outcomes. For one such examination, see Jake Harwood and Lisa Sparks, "Social Identity and Health: Intergroup Communication Approach to Cancer," *Health Communication* 15:2 (2003), 145–59.

52 Susan Sontag, *Illness as Metaphor* (New York: Farrar, Straus and Giroux, 1978), 3.

53 Hitchens, *Mortality*, 3.

54 Ibid.

55 Ibid., 28.

56 Gubar, *Memoir of a Debulked Woman*, 89.

57 Gubar, *Reading & Writing Cancer*, preface.

58 Ibid.

59 Kelly Corrigan, *The Middle Place* (New York: Hyperion, 2008), 154.

60 Ibid.

61 Meghan O'Rourke, *The Long Goodbye* (New York: Riverhead Books, 2011), 88–89.

62 Jain, *Malignant*, 3.

63 Hitchens, *Mortality*, 11.

64 Radner, *It's Always Something*, 206.

65 "Leading Causes of Death," National Center for Health Statistics, Centers for Disease Control and Prevention, http://www.cdc.gov/nchs/fastats/leading-causes-of-death.htm. "Deaths Registered in England and Wales: 2015," Office for National Statistics, https://www.ons.gov.uk/peoplepopulationandcommunity/births deathsandmarriages/deaths/bulletins/deathsregistrationsummarytables/2015.

Chapter 4

1 "Mammogram Basics," American Cancer Society, http://www.cancer.org/healthy/findcancerearly/examandtestdescriptions/mammogramsandotherbreastimagingprocedures/mammograms-and-other-breast-imaging-procedures-what-is-mammogram.

2 "Breast Cancer Screening (PDQ)," National Cancer Institute, https://www.cancer.gov/types/breast/hp/breast-screening-pdq#section/all.

3 Ibid.

4 Ibid.

5 Ibid.

6 Christie Aschwanden, "I'm Just Saying No to Mammography: Why the Numbers Are in My Favor," *The Washington Post*, October 7, 2013, https://www.washingtonpost.com/national/health-science/im-just-saying-no-to-mammography-why-the-numbers-are-in-my-favor/2013/10/07/733c0894-29e1-11e3-8ade-a1f23cda135e_story.html.

7 Paul Ehrlich, "Partial Cell Functions," Nobel lecture, December 11, 1908, 304–20, http://www.nobelprize.org/nobel_prizes/medicine/laureates/1908/ehrlich-lecture.pdf.

8 Ibid.

9 Vincent T. DeVita and Elizabeth DeVita-Raeburn, *The Death of Cancer* (New York: Farrar, Straus and Giroux, 2015), 108.

10 Ibid., 105.

11 Ibid., 68–69.

12 "Chemotherapy for Hodgkin Disease," American Cancer Society, https://www.cancer.org/cancer/hodgkin-lymphoma/treating/chemotherapy.html

13 Ibid., 17.

14 Gawande, *Being Mortal*, 167.

15 Ibid., 167–68.

16 DeVita and DeVita-Raeburn, *The Death of Cancer*, 26.

17 Gawande, *Being Mortal*, 177.

18 DeVita and DeVita-Raeburn, *The Death of Cancer*, 27.

19 Thierry Conroy et al., "FOLFIRINOX versus Gemcitabine for Metastatic Pancreatic Cancer," *New England Journal of*

Medicine 364 (May 12, 2011): 1817–25, http://www.nejm.org/doi/full/10.1056/NEJMoa1011923.

20 "Information for Health Care Providers," Centers for Disease Control, http://www.cdc.gov/cancer/preventinfections/providers.htm.

21 Rhonda Pickett, email, February 19, 2015.

22 Ibid.

23 Donna D. Ignatavicius and M. Linda Workman, *Medical-Surgical Nursing: Patient-Centered Collaborative Care* (Amsterdam: Elsevier Health Sciences, 2015), 196.

24 Patricia Grace King, "The Cancer Diaries: Week Two," June 21, 2014, http://www.patriciagraceking.com/uncategorized/the-cancer-diaries-week-two/.

Chapter 5

1 "Health Effects of the Chernobyl Accident: An Overview," World Health Organization, April 2006, http://www.who.int/ionizing_radiation/chernobyl/backgrounder/en/.

2 Jimmy Carter, *Why Not the Best? The First Fifty Years*, reprint (Fayetteville, AR: University of Arkansas Press, 1996), 54.

3 Ibid.

4 Denise Grady, "In a Former First Family, Cancer Has a Grim Legacy," *New York Times*, August 7, 2007, http://www.nytimes.com/2007/08/07/health/07jimm.html.

5 Erwin Schrödinger, *What Is Life?*, 1944 (Cambridge, UK: Cambridge University Press, 2012), 1.

6 Carina Storrs, "How Much Do CT Scans Increase the Risk of Cancer?" *Scientific American*, July 1, 2013, https://www.scientificamerican.com/article/how-much-ct-scans-increase-risk-cancer/.

7 Ibid.

8 Ibid.

9 Nicholas Palvidis, Georgio Stanta, and Riccardo A. Audisio, "Cancer Prevalence and Mortality in Centarians: A Systemic Review," *Clinical Review of Oncological Hematology* 83:1 (July 2012), 145–52, https://www.ncbi.nlm.nih.gov/pubmed/22024388.

10 "Survival Rates for Melanoma Skin Cancer, by Stage," American Cancer Society, http://www.cancer.org/cancer/skincancer-melanoma/detailedguide/melanoma-skin-cancer-survival-rates-by-stage.

11 Linda Marsa, "Immunotherapy's Promise Against Cancer," *U.S. News and World Report*, October 6, 2015, http://health.usnews.com/health-news/patient-advice/articles/2015/10/06/immunotherapys-promise-against-cancer.

12 Andy Coghlan, "Cancer's Penicillin Moment: Drugs that Unleash the Immune System," *New Scientist*, March 2, 2016, https://www.newscientist.com/article/2078956-cancers-penicillin-moment-drugs-that-unleash-the-immune-system/.

13 Rhonda Pickett, email, October 13, 2016.

14 DeVita and DeVita-Raeburn, *The Death of Cancer*, 252.

15 Domenico Napolitani, Michelle Signore, and Daniele C. Struppa, "Cancer Quasispecies and Stem-like Adaptive Aneuploidy," *F1000Research* 2 (December 2013), 268.

16 Danely P. Slaughter, Harry W. Southwick, and Walter Smejkal, "'Field Cancerization' in Oral Stratified Squamous Epithelium,"

Cancer 6 (September 1953), 963–68, http://onlinelibrary.wiley. com/store/10.1002/1097-0142(195309)6:5%3C963::AID-CNCR2820060515%3E3.0.CO;2-Q/asset/2820060515_ftp.pdf?v =1&t=iufl1ugj&s=bd2f274c75ceaca14c00f0932bf9a1a3609db96f.

17 "Provocative Questions," National Cancer Institute, https:// provocativequestions.nci.nih.gov/rfa/mainquestions_listview. html.

18 Ibid.

19 Ibid.

20 Katy J. L. Bell, Chris Del Mar, Gordon Wright, James Dickinson, and Paul Glasziou, "Prevalence of Incidental Prostate Cancer: A Systematic Review of Autopsy Studies," *International Journal of Cancer* 137: 7, 1749–57, http:// onlinelibrary.wiley.com/doi/10.1002/ijc.29538/full.

21 Janina Marguc, Jens Förster, and Gerben A. Van Kleef, "Stepping Back to See the Big Picture: When Obstacles Elicit Global Processing," *The Journal of Personality and Social Psychology* 101:5 (November 2011), 883–901.

22 Jeannine Gailey, "When My Doctor Said, 'We're Lucky We Found the Cancer,'" *The Mighty*, August 12, 2016, https:// themighty.com/2016/08/does-luck-play-a-role-in-receiving-a-carcinoid-syndrome-diagnosis/.

23 Lucille Clifton, "1994," Poetry Foundation, https://www. poetryfoundation.org/poems-and-poets/poems/detail/49490.

24 Audre Lorde, *The Cancer Journals*, Aunt Lute Books, 1980.

25 Ibid.

26 Gubar, *Reading & Writing Cancer*, 31.

27 Charles and Ray Eames (writers and directors), *Powers of Ten*, IBM Distribution, 1977, https://www.youtube.com/ watch?v=0fKBhvDjuy0.

INDEX

Page references for illustrations appear in *italics*.